THE WATER GARDEN

An anthology of poems by Sally E Dalglish, friends and guides

Illustrations from the original paintings by Sally E. Dalglish

Visit us online at www.authorsonline.co.uk

An AuthorsOnLine Book

Copyright © Authors OnLine Ltd 2004

Text Copyright © Sally Dalglish 2004

Cover design by Sally Dalglish ©

All illustrations by Sally Dalglish ©

All rights reserved. No part of this publication may be reproduced, stored in a retrieval system, or transmitted in any form or by any means, electronic, mechanical, photocopy, recording or otherwise, without prior written permission of the copyright owner. Nor can it be circulated in any form of binding or cover other than that in which it is published and without similar condition including this condition being imposed on a subsequent purchaser.

ISBN 0 7552 0126 4

Authors OnLine Ltd
40 Castle Street
Hertford SG14 1HR
England

This book is also available in e-book format, details of which are available at www.authorsonline.co.uk

Sally Dalglish spent her formative years in West Sussex. She attended St. Mary's School, Calne and Bradford University, editing *Universification*. In 1973 she travelled overland to India with John France. They married on November 14th 1973 and parted in 1982. Sally taught for 3 years before returning to Sussex to learn to repair oriental rugs, her present occupation.

She has a deep love of the country and of gardening and enjoys fell-walking, swimming and sculpture.

dedicated to
the voice of H.R.H. The Prince of Wales,
a portcullissed messiah,
President of WaterAid.

To Kay,

the revered willow in the water garden

love from

Sally

The Water Garden — SECTION I — Sally Dalglish

1. Drip — 1
2. Vessel — 2
3. Song of the sea — 4
4. Caught — 5
5. Sobs for Pops — 6
6. My cell — 7
7. Credo — 8
8. We Are the Universe — 10
9. Le Blaireau et le Saule Pleureur — 12
10. Il Est Defendu — 13
11. On Seeing — 14
11. Death Glory — 15
11. Moonlit Catch — 16
14. Keeping up with Mr. Griswold-Jones — 17
15. Feed-Time — 18
16. Advert for a Bathroom — 19
17. A Growing Silence in the Thickets — 21
18. Joss — 23
20. Lavache — 24
21. It could Have Been You — 25
19. Ragbone Man — 27
22. Oh Y-faced Cat! — 29
26. Friend Come — 31
27. Moonshine Monster — 33
28. Ode to Tiger Cherub Og Mog — 34
29. Post Round — 35
30. Your Thousandth Mile — 37
23. Under the Trees — 38
21. Apostrophe to a Young Alsation — 39

24.	Snow Watch	40
31.	Dam Square	41
32.	Strangers Passing on a Train	43
33.	Till Cobwebs Cover the Sky	45
34.	Supplication	47
35.	O Fishes	71
36.	Ignorance	48
37.	Difficulty of Getting Through	49
38.	May 13th Ten Years On	50
39.	Fleeced By Night	51
40.	Perspective	53
41.	The Place Where I live	54
42.	Praise for the Grey Days	55
43.	Folkestone	56
44.	Souvenir	57
45.	My Tabernacle	59
46.	Braithwaite Moss	60
47.	Collar Dove	61
48.	The Doormat	63
49.	The Note Under the Mat	65
50.	A Change on the Face	67
51.	Not So Lucky	68
52.	Tranquillity	72
53.	Yena Couja!	73
54.	The Lotus Flower	74
55.	What do I now Believe?	76
56.	Blaeberry Fell	78
57.	Old Man Oak	79
58.	Water in a Fly's Eye	82
59.	Waller Brook Dartmoor 1957	83
60.	Water is my God	84
61.	End of the Rainbow	85

62. Tearing the Ocean Down		86
63. Heretical Fish		87
64. The Source		89

The Water Garden	SECTION II	WaterAid
1. Tijan M. Sallah -	Sahelian Earth	91
2. Adam Barratt (13)	Picture yourself	93
3. Enid Katorobo -	The little girl at the tap	94
4.	Sweet sweet water	96
5.	If	97
Class 9 Horton Grange First School in Blyth -		
6.	Water! A plea for those without	99
7. Gareth Wilson (15)	Water can be	101
8. Benjamin Hopwood (8)	Oh no! It's raining again	102
9. Terry Marston	The Umbrella Seller	103
10. David Hodges	Delayed By Rough Seas	105
11.	The Sea, The Sea	107
12.	Nature Notes	110
13.	Pilgrimage	192
14.	Wilderness	112
15.	A Winter Sunset	113
16.	The Playfulness of God	114
17.	Birds migrating South	116
18.	Rock Pool	117
19.	Nothing in November	119
20.	The Mystic Path	121
21.	WaterAid	122
22. Zena Huggar	Water for All –who cares?	123

The Water Garden   SECTION III   Friends and Guides

1. Les Marchant, (1906-2000) dear friend and guide		
	Seeded Universe	126
2. Lyn Birkbeck, astrologer and guide		
	The Wave	127
3. Jelaluddin Rumi, spiritual guide		
	Mathnawi I, 3555-8	129
4. (1207-1273)	II, 566-8	130
5.	II, 716-8	131
6.	II, 1020-1	132
7.	II, 3296-3302	133
8. Lao-tze, Old Master	Tao Te Ching	
	ch 8 Easy by Nature (circa 500 BC)	134
9.	ch.15 People of Power Cc 500 (BC)	135
10.	ch 78 Paradoxes (circa 500 B.C.)	136
11. Dawne Kovan	Haiku: Who Sees?	137
12.	Tanka: Kyoto Temple	137
13. Angela Locke	Sacred Earth	138
14.	Crab Skeleton	140
15.	Rose in Stone	142
16.	Iona	146
17.	Whales off the North beach: Iona	148
18.	Earth Music	150
19.	Himalayan Rainbow	152
20.	Bay Horse Farm	153
21.	Martindale Picnic	155
22.	Disturbing the Heron	157
23.	Tarn	159
24. Mary Burkett O.B.E.	The Mist	161
25.	The River Derwent	162
26.	Driving over Dunmail after a Storm	162

27.		Seascale	163
28. Geraldine Green		We Walk the Land	164
29.		I rescued four baby newts	166
30.		Remember the gods of small places	167
31.		In one Field	168
32. Geraldine Green		Sal Madge	170
33.		Tupping-time	171
34.		Solway	172
35. Dennis Irwin		Watersmeet	173
36. Mike Brown A.E (dear flying friend of Charles Dalglish)		Free Spirit, High Flier	175
37. Faye Dalglish		In memory of Alex Dalglish	178
38. Norma Gunn		A Time to grieve	179
39.		Reflections and Echoes	180
40.		Dark Horizon	181
41. Patricia Irwin		Magic	182
42. Jonathan Atkinson		Aquifer	183
43. John Crossley		Rain	184
44. Charles Gardiner		River of Dreams	185
45. Jane Moss-Luffrum		The Drowning	187
46. Huw Evans		Fewer Mouths	189
47. Dorothy Chalk		The Colour of Sound	190
48.		The Monster Serpent	191
49.		Pilgrimage	192
50.		Safe Harbour	194
51.		What do we hear?	196
52. Jill Jackson		Green Chakra	198
53.		Regeneration	199
54. Hazel Lee		The Pull of Water	200
55. Alicia Lester		Inside the Shell	202
56. Margaret Morton		Water of Life	203
57. Vi Taylor		The Sea	204

58. Ann Ward	Archaeologist's Report: 4000 AD	206
59. Sylvia Stevens	Sea-Beast	207
60. Elizabeth Josh	Aira Force	208
61.	Memory	209
62.	The Quiet Pool	210
63.	Raindrops on the Window	211
64.	The Stream Spoke to Me	212

List of Illustrations

No. Poem	Illustration	Page
Section I		
2. Vessel	Vessels	3
8. We are the Universe	Transformation	11
22. Oh Y faced Cat!	A Cat may look at a King	30
33. Till Cobwebs Cover the Sky	From the Spider's Web	46
54. The Lotus Flower	The Lotus Flowers	75
57. Old Man Oak	Old Man Oak	81
63. Heretical Fish	Heretical Fish	88
Section II		
4. If	A Bucket of Dreams	98
11. The Sea, the Sea	We came from the Sea	109
18. Rock Pool	Rock Pool	118
Section III		
15. Rose in Stone	Rose in Stone	145
28. We Walk the Land	We Walk the Land	165
31. In One Field	I am Each of These	169
35. Watersmeet	The Meeting of Magnificent and Delightful	174
45. The Drowning	In Death We Reach All	188
54. The Pull of Water	The Pull of Water	201
64. The Stream Spoke to me	The Plight of Water	213

Front Cover: The Water Garden

The illustrations are taken from a collection of symbolic water colours by Sally E. Dalglish

ACKNOWLEDGEMENTS

The compiler gratefully acknowledges the poets themselves, as well as the following copyright holders, for their kind permission to reprint the poems in this anthology.

Five poems: I, 3555-8, II, 566-8, II, 716-8, II, 1020-1, II, 3296-3302 from RUMI DAYLIGHT: A Daybook of Spiritual Guidance, translated by Camille & Kabir Helminski. Copyright 1994 by Camille & Helminski. Reprinted by arrangement with Shambhala Publications, Inc., Boston, www.shambhala.com

"Easy by nature," "People of power" and "Paradoxes" from LAO TZU: TAO TEH CHING by Ursula K. Leguin. Copyright 1997 by Ursula K. Leguin. Reprinted by arrangement with Shambhala Publications, Inc., Boston, www.shambhala.com

Lyn Birkbeck, "The Wave." Copyright 1994 Lyn Birkbeck

Mary E. Burkett O.B.E. "The Mist," "The River Derwent," "Driving over Dunmail after a Storm" and "Seascale." Copyright Mary E. Burkett

Sally Dalglish: poems 1-64 in Section I are all Copyright 2003 Sally E. Dalglish

Geraldine Green, "Remember the gods of small places," "I rescued four baby newts," "In one field" and "We walk the land" from *The Skin* edited by Charles Johnson. Copyright 2003 by Geraldine Green. Reprinted with permission of Flarestack Publishing.

Geraldine Green, "Solway" in *Cumbria* Magazine edited by Terry Fletcher. Copyright 2000 Geraldine Green. "Sal Madge" copyright 2000 Geraldine Green. "Tupping-time" from *Envoi* poetry magazine edited by Roger Elkin. Copyright 2000 Geraldine Green.

Angela Locke, "Bay Horse Farm," "Martindale Picnic," "Disturbing the Heron" and "Tarn" from *North Face*. Copyright 1989 Angela Locke. Reprinted with permission from Pleiades Press.

Angela Locke, "Sacred Earth," "Crab Skeleton," "Rose in Stone," "Iona," "Whales off the North Beach: Iona," "Earth Music" and "Himalayan Rainbow" from *Sacred Earth*. Copyright 2001 Angela Locke. Reprinted with permission from Pleides Press.

Tijan M. Sallah, "Sahelian Earth," from *African New Voices* Copyright Tijan M. Sallah

Adam Barratt, "Water". Poem supplied by courtesy of Severn Trent Water.
Benjamin Hopwood, "Raining again." Poem supplied by courtesy of Severn Trent Water.
Gareth Wilson, "Water Can Be." Poem supplied by courtesy of Severn Trent Water.

While every effort has been made to trace and acknowledge copyright holders, the compiler has not been successful in all cases but has decided nevertheless to publish the poems with the intent of exposing the poet's works and advancing their reputations. Queries and corrections are welcome so that future editions can be amended.

Special thanks go to Wendy Bonington, Fiona Cox, Geraldine Green, Norma Gunn, Eileen Lilburn, Angela Locke and The Mungrisedale Poets; Les Marchant; Rebecca Wood - the fund-raising manager at WaterAid; The Straight Arrow Lodge and to Will Fuller who provided the computer and the necessary technical expertise.

INTRODUCTION

My grandmother used to wash up for the three of us in a teacup of water. Each morning she would splash her face in half a cup. When asked why she was so sparing with water she replied, "It's so precious, isn't it?"

That wisdom prompted me to write my Will entirely in favour of WaterAid.

The earth is a water garden and within its confines are streets and cities, springs and oceans. The earth's surface is 75% water. You are 75% water. Water is not always obvious: it has an unlimited capacity for form-creation and metamorphosis.

Water is the most receptive substance in existence. According to Masaru Emoto in *Messages from Water*, water reflects people's consciousness. Just by expressing love and gratitude, the water around us and in our bodies changes so beautifully (as illustrated by crystal photography.) Water appears to be the soul of this being, Earth.

The human body is a hydro-electric system but one which cannot easily function in perfect health unless given 8-10 glasses of tap water and half a teaspoon of sea-salt daily according to Dr. Batmanghelidj in *Water and Salt – your healers from within*. His research has shown that most ailments, pain and diseases are caused by chronic dehydration. And, of course, coffee, tea, sodas and alcohol all dehydrate. As water gardens we are filling ourselves with chemicals and fluids that no bird, plant or animal could tolerate. But we know best. Water and salt taken half an hour before meals and two and a half hours after are possibly the only cure for most allergies and diseases. No drug ever appears to have actually cured anyone.

The Water Garden contains three sections and 18 symbolic water colours. In my section water is not often obvious. It may appear fleetingly in a host of disguises from a drip to a kiss, a tear or a splash. But the central section contains poems collected by WaterAid from Africans who know the extremity of being without water; schoolchildren in their earliest days of compassion for those who lack water and poems from a monk who lives by the sea.

The third section contains poetry from friends and guides. It has its origins in China, Afghanistan, Australia and Cumbria, spanning 2,500 years. Each of these poems has shaped my outlook.

To me water is more valuable than all the fruits of economic progress. It is the source of life, the healer, a sacred element, largely abused and desecrated. When Mars was closest to the Earth in 2003 we were encouraged by the astrologers to voice our deepest wish. Mine is to see a universal reverence for water.

Sally E. Dalglish 2004

The Water Garden

Section 1

Sally Dalglish

Drip
June '63

He slouches down the dim-lit street
And shadows slip beneath his feet
He stops to stare across the road
And sees a girl who soon is gone
So turns again, his head is lowered
A moment waits then passes on.

To the door of a pub he makes his way
There he stays at the bar to pay
For each drink he takes. No man gives him
a free pint, no-one laughs with him
Or talks and shares his thoughts so dim
For he's alone his life is grim.

Cold night entombs the city dead
Each foggy lamp-post hangs its head
While shedding light o'er all the town
The gawk comes through the streets, resigned
He stalks towards a bend - no sound
Disturbs his solitary mind.

Sally Dalglish [aged 14]   Calne

Vessel   1965

I am an eyeless vessel
Into which
You and the world pour
What you will
I cannot see the contents
That are within me

But you
You are a cistern
Forever filling and refilling yourself
With fresh waters.

Sally Dalglish (aged 15)

Vessels Sally Dalglish

Song of the Sea   1964

I know he's there
He's come back once again for me
I'll go down by the sea
And he'll be there.

He went away
He never said goodbye to me that day
I thought I'd lost him for aye
But now he's back.

I know he's there
He's come back once again for me
I'll go down by the sea
And he'll be there.

Sally Dalglish   Heyshott, Sussex

Caught

7th July '65

A pearly sea-shell on the shore
Holds me within its walls
Myriad patterns
Cover a surface
That I in the gloom cannot see.
For inside it is dark and empty
Where there was light before.

Would God that the sea
Might gather it up
And toss me upon the waves!
Would God I were free
From its cavity
To sail on its back and gaze
At its million designs.

Sally Dalglish

Sobs for Pops   July 1965

Dear friend I mourn thy loss No longer can we exercise
Our power complex on thy petite self
Nor shall we hear some quaint remark
From you, and smile thus cheered the while.
Nor shall our room without you be complete
Each walk without you shall deficient be
Each meal shall lack some spirit for your loss

But visit us remembering to bring
Some succulent choice gifts to keep the starved
Replenished and we shall not then forget
The Bygone Days, recalling from the past
The pleasanter memories to wit.
Write to us all and we will surely do
Likewise. And when perchance it rains
At half past two think of us soaked
Upon the pitch in games.

Sally Dalglish   St. Mary's, Calne

My Cell   February '66

A distant whisper from the desert where the cactus grows
Floats meaningless across my wan and lurid prison cell
How many hours and days and nights have passed I cannot tell
How long this endless still will last, God only knows.
Oh for some stormy torrent to disrupt the gentleness
There is no gentleness in crime. For me a murderess
Retribution came too soon; with half a life to go
So young for death, I hate all young things now.

Sally Dalglish

Credo   March 68

I believe

In a unifying force with which
Only beings who are free to choose
Have consciously disharmonised.

Every blade of Nature is controlled
By a single master mind.

It grows from the ground
Thrives in the air
And is buried to resurge again

It repeats itself with rhythm
Its apparent discords harmonise
The music of Nature!
The music of the ground
The music of the air
The music of the water
The music of the fire.

Listen to the woods
The trees, the plants, the grass
To the produce of the earth.

Listen to the air
The whisperings, moanings, howlings of the wind
To all who breathe in it.

Listen on the seashore
To the splash or lashings of the sea,
On the bank
To the trickle, fall or silent pressing
Of the water in the pool

Listen by the chimney
To the roaring up the wall
To the murmur in the fireplace
Or the crackling, whistling, humming logs
That flare up as they fall,

And ask why man made music:
So that he should share it all
And know one mind behind the harmony
Created all.

Sally Dalglish

We Are the Universe   17 April '68

When two spheres drift apart
And their warmth is grown cold
And space is once more, not a dream, but a void
Then take my soul again to the heights
On some other planet of death
Only there can I find the sweet paradise
of your breath.

When Venus and Mars meet on their solar path
Then let them unite, for two lesser worlds
Would give them faint joy not harmony
A diminished power would cloudier prove
Duller than the beauty of their love

Twilight creeps over the universe.
A profounder blue stirs the deeper sands of the sea
We struggle on earth float on the ocean
And fly through the air to where
No lone person will ever fly

Sally Dalglish   Paris

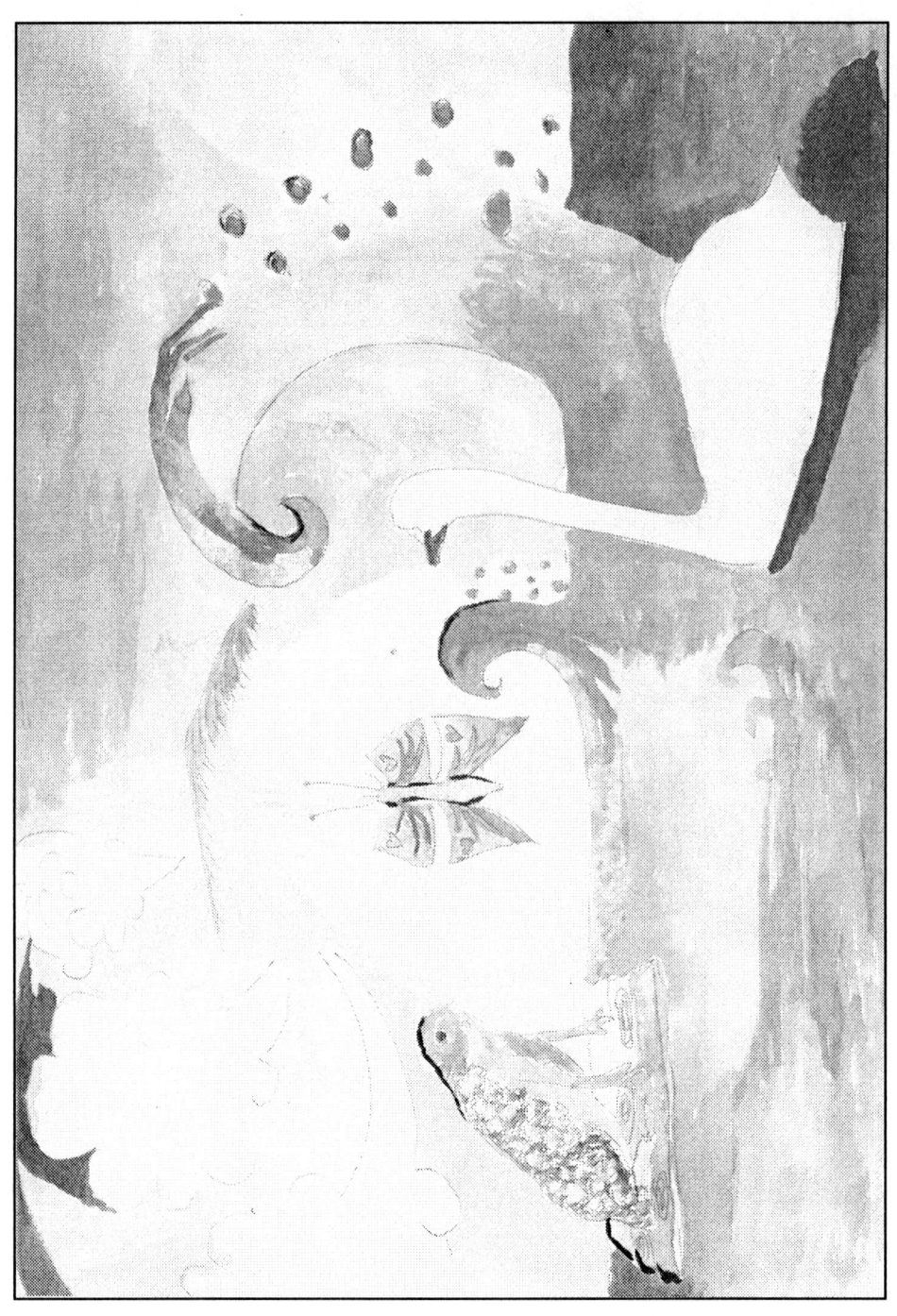

Transformation by Sally Dalglish

Le Blaireau et le Saule pleureur   18 April 1968

Les feuilles qui egaillent le saule pleureur
Sont eparpillees par le brise du coeur;
Comme les rayons du soleil sont emousses
Par les feuilles fremissantes qui tremoussaient
Le blaireau noir flane le long de la rive.
Il sort chaque soir, une bete tres active
Le romantique, qui cherche son ivresse
Chez l'arbre seul, pour adoucir sa tristesse.

Berce dans le giron du saule pluereur
Dans ses pattes noires et blanches une seule fleur
Le blaireau partage avec l'arbre: une joie –
Une extase rehausee par la brise. De loin
Revient le blaireau, l'arbre demure
Mais jamais ne sont-ils divises au couer
Comme le fleur coule toujours inepuise
Les feuilles souhaitent toujours sur les brisees.

Sally Dalglish   Sorbonne

Il Est Defendu　　　　　　April 1968

Il est defendu de cracher sur le trottoir.
Ne passez pas ici.
Point de poisons jusqu'au demain.
Ne pas pencher hors de la fenetre.
Il faut que vous faites un detour.
Jamais criez "au secours!" parce qu'il est trop tard.
Ne touchez pas.

I would not touch nor spit nor lean nor shout nor
Buy my fish from you
I'll take the detour, cross a different way
Eat eggs and smile when I fall down or drown

I'll not defile your clean and lovely pavements
With my rank spittal
Effervescing with typhoid
Cancer, mumps, diphtheria.
Don't want yer fish –
My only wish would be
To write a note beside
Saying: "Touchez! Crachez!
Penchez! Criez! Quelque place
que vous voulez.
Do what you want to do
And do it now

Sally Dalglish　　　　　　　　　　　　　　　　Paris

On Seeing   25 May '68

My eye's glazed as the water's skin
Are mocked by the crow
Preening his appearance
On the peak of the fir
Dazzled by pastel colours
Shaken by this colour they call green
Everything that is not what they call
Pink and blue and yellow
And what I know is Black
Is green green green
"Agreable," I learnt that word in Braille.

My fingers have been my life
And it was black
Real but lightless
And they tell me that colour is green
And I feel dizzy
My stomach retches
I have seen too much in one minute
I have laughed and wept
To see so much colour
And so much green.

Sally Dalglish   Chichester

Death Glory   11 April '68

The magnificence of dying
Before the desertion of winter
Is complete!
Warm reynard bracken moor slopes
Brilliant leaves lisping to the ground
And red spatterings
Of toadstool mouldy posts
Bright berries
Resilient in the wind I see
A denuded twig
Jerking over the constant stream –
I laugh at the eternity of things
The harmony and order
Unquestioning re-occurrence
Modulated repetition
As the renewed tree every year
Follows the same pattern
While I seeking harmony and order
Unity and purpose
Light and understanding
Ask: why?

Sally Dalglish   Admergill, Blacko

Moonlit Catch   November 1968

At dusk the cat prowls by the fungus stump
Beside the tentacles of silver
On the cobweb ridden dank barn door
Slinks across the stone slab by the stream
Pauses, flashes his white whiskers
And darts in mad pursuit of leaves.
The chill round moon gleams unveiled
Cat makes his lunar vigil.

The frost-crusted grass makes no sound
Under his padded feet.
His senses taut, poised he anticipates his sport;
He stops, sneaks to the left,
Pounces on his squeaking prey
Then the torment, the playful tease
And the feast
To the last hair of the mouse's tail.

Sally Dalglish   Admergill Hall

Keeping Up With Mr Griswold-Jones 10 November '68

To purgatory with the man who views his colour TV
By the window and leaves the curtains open wide
For all the jealous passers-by to see.
Who prevaricates about the boiled fish you've spied
With, "Of course we usually have steak for tea."
He'd say anything to keep his pride.

Should he meet you by surprise one morning
when he's out
In his wife's tatty morris traveller, he'll
excuse the fact –
With , "The jag's at the garage – they lent me
this to get about."
"How's business?" you enquire with tact
For you know that he's not working, but he'll
quickly slay your doubt;
You'd never dream a man of his importance
had been, sacked.

Sally Dalglish   Trawden, Lancashire

Feed-Time
19 June 1969

Greedy billed birds green-headed and plump
Waddle and quack in the sun
Pirouette – one leg one wing outstretched
Plash! Land in the pond
Paddle slowly away on the waves
And plummet the depths for grubs

Swans thunder the length of the pond
Feet pacing, wings beat necks are craned
Then halt, dip curved necks up and down
To sip water, refresh and preen again

Great geese gambol along after food
Heads lurching forward in search
Grass-eaters, red-eyed, red-billed
Surly-faced but not fierce
All gulp down white bread crusts and buns
And snatch from the hands of a child

Mighty family owners of this slime-ridden
Pond-weedy patch, pulling each other's feathers
Gurgling and hissing, flapping and swimming
For you life's one idle feast.

Sally Dalglish   Midhurst

16.

Advert for a Bathroom in a Small Inn   9 September '69

Please take this room
Away from me – you'll have
Pink peeling walls through which
A more ancient cream is visible;
Pipes encircling the perimeter
And running up the wall;
Underfoot, green lino, half streaked
Which would surely curl up
To behold the bottom of a brush

Near, but not against two walls
A shapely bath on lion's claws
Stands complete with chain enclosed
By a clanging pipe to plug the hole;
And at one end of the room
A rumbling sliding door
[As in a farmyard dairy]
Partially conceals strange, flat smells
Of musty trunks and disused clothes

Splash bespattered walls are left unwiped.
The spider makes his web quite undisturbed.
The white lace curtain gathers grey.
The mirror, specs of an economy
Talcum powder, shaving cream and dust.
Weather and steam in counter-attack

Have swelled the window frame firm shut
While perpetual naked feet have shrunk
The loose-threaded bathroom mat

In the rubble of the creaking shelf
A flat-headed bristle-bent red toothbrush
Sits in a nibbled plastic mug.
A topless tube of toothpaste
Adorns the nivea in gateau fashion.
You feel the filth is permanent
And if you were forced to stay there
Half an hour, you would reappear
Full thirty minutes dirtier.

Sally Dalglish

A Growing Silence in the Thickets   April '70

Matchless serenity of the dead leaves
And mildly waving briar,
Calm thorn, cool grass, still trees!
Each hazel branch waits patiently
Anticipating the painless birth
Of a new leaf, another life.
Each placid puddle gazes upward
At the changeless clouded sky
And all the while, the waiting and the peace
Conceal the almighty birth of Spring.

King birds: radiant cock pheasants
Strut with their dowdy wives;
Young scampering rabbits
Dart away in the undergrowth;
Light thrush and dark blackbird –
Both sing their loving songs
While the perky sparrow,
As forward as ever,
Undaunted by changing seasons
Chirps his own air.

Drops of rain begin to moisten
The parted lips of grass.
The lisping stings of nettles
And tangled thickets, wicker work

Of untouched stalks decaying.
A sudden shriek I hear:
Another pheasant warns his mates,
For all is not free of fear,
I, the intruder, am here;
Caught in the movement of Spring.

Sally Dalglish　　　　　　　　　　　　　　　　　　　　　　Sussex

Joss   21 June 1970

You will never gaze at me
Until our eyes meet
You lick me with your tongue
You touch my feet
I stroke your fine black head
You rest your head
Upon my crouching shoulder
Every year you grow five older
While I stay young and love you still
What kind of dog are you
To make my eyes with water fill?
Joss, my dog, I love you.

Sally Dalglish   Admergill

Lavache 9 October '70

We are not great men as we thought we'd be
Not heroes in our home or working hours
Nor Valentinos between the sheets
Nor Shakespeare in our written word
Nor Madonnas in our motherhood

We dream of stopping wars
Of halting death, disease and age
Of being Maecenas to the arts
Mahatma in great mysteries
And alchemist in our discoveries.

In dreams I've sailed the seas
Won every combat I've gained every goal
For real I am Amphitryon
The entertainer, no Aphrodite
To your love, but Lavache –
Life's obscurest clown.

Sally Dalglish

It Could Have Been You 11 November '70

Does it disturb you that she fell?
It could have been you

Like a stone plummeting in the water
She fell – the radii of ripples
Will touch so many people – not just
Her friends and family, but you and me
Why did we drive her to die
People like you and me?

Somebody thought it a dummy
Hurtling past the glass
I thought it was someone sleeping
On the balcony – until I saw
Her hands were blue
Who urged her to it – you?

Poison she took and slashed her wrists
But what did she feel – lost?
Lost, anomic, alien in a city where
She was just another "student"
In a throng of faceless students
People as communicative as you or me.

Grieve for de Gaulle, grieve and mourn
His life was full and now he's gone
But remember Doreen who will never grow old
Who has loved and been loved, lived and died
Does it disturb you that she fell?
It could have been you.

Sally Dalglish   Bradford

Ragbone Man   18 November 1970

You thrash the cat and belt the dog
And tie your ragbone pony to a tree
You heap the grease fat ridden pans
On grandma's knitting when it's you she's knitting for

Each night you fill your inebriated belly
With the grub the kids could well have eaten
Tomorrow. You bang the doors you kick
The tatty chairs and stumble into bed.

Half dead you start on me –
More an attack than amorous
The kids toss and whimper in the night
The street lamps burn – you sleep.

And in the morning – when the window's black
It's grey in daytime, peeling, rotten, damp –
You throw the clothes off and put on your own
Set off to work up on your ragbone cart.

"Ragbone" you shout from one street to the next
And stop and collect a priceless skull
Some priceless idiot found attached
To a mouse's skeleton in the cellar.

"Ragbone!" you shout and get a jacket here
A water butt, an iron, a box of screws
Some knickers, trousers, hats with holes
Old curtains, an odd pair of shoes.

And in the evening when you've fed your pony
And tied him choking to a tree, you'll slouch off
To drink and throw your darts
Then you'll come back to me.

Sally Dalglish   Bradford

Oh Y-faced Cat   1971

Oh Y-faced cat of cats
With sunshine eyes
And ears the size of bats'
Your purring is birdsong in my ear
Your dewdrop smile
Your gentle paws
Delight me
Your shivering back
And quivering tail
Invite me
To caress your fur
And scratch your stuck-out chin.

Sally Dalglish   Rooley Lane

A Cat may look at a King by Sally Dalglish

Friend Come   13 January 1971

I have nodded my head and shaken my brow
Browsing through liberal Forum articles
While Joan Baez sings porously on
And I have warmed my mulled wine
Legs beside the three red bars
And murmured half-remembered songs
Into my Brazilian coffee dregs
And I have prepared to exude
Some lines and gurgitate strong words
From the nexus of my pen
With the monotonous wide-lined paper.

I gaze at the fractured fence
The cat's grave, the sauntering cinematic
Passers-by, the progression and recession
Of traffic wheels and sounds:
All these reverberate against my vision
Through five-eighth shuttered windows
And these succinct white net curtains.

The days draw in and we must too
Our chairs and belts — what the hell for?
This is a question on which I expect you
To write 1,760 words and place them
At yard intervals down Wakefield Road
So that the Indian conductor, Moo,
Will know that the English mile shall reign
Supreme over Punjab and Bombay

And all the Ganges ducks of the world.

My friend will come, my friend will come
And see me tipping ash upon my knee
Because I hate mulled red wine
Tights but I said that I would wear them
Till they went to holes.

My friend has come
The splashing wheels can go on by
I shall go and put on reggae
And we will close the shutters
And brew another can of coffee
For us all. And together we will go
To Nirvana, me, you and your myrmidons.

Sally Dalglish   Bradford

Moonshine Monster   13 January 1971

Moonshine you come alive at night
Your mind is slick as water
You are the opportunist
Your words convince me
That what I'm doing must be wrong
But still I aid you when you ask.

You spin from business to more business
In the early hours of dawn
You lie unconscious till it's noon
Then fly from one town to another
Doing business and more business
Never tiring, rarely seen to eat
Always driving, always got some man to meet
Questions I ask you
You evade them all
Or hurl such plausible explanations
In my face
That I retire awhile.

You, the slick skinhead
You, the dark monster of my dreams
You, the wide brown-eyed beauty
With vitality and zest, you
Bewitch me with your voice, your smiles and charm.

Sally Dalglish

Ode to Tiger Cherub Og-Mog   30 January 1971

Poor little scrat cat
Scraggy as a drowning rat
Now your fleas will all be gone
With the dettol you've got on

Pretty pathetic little mog
Tail all stringy, eyes agog
Suffering the damp aftermath
Of an unmewed for bloody bath

The pained expression in those eyes
Mixed with indignation and surprise
As you walk rockily, shaking each paw
And steam beside the fire on the floor

Poor little scrat cat
Scraggy as a mountain rat
Your fleas are dead and you've been sick
Wasn't that bath a dirty trick?

Sally Dalglish

Post Round   1 February 1971
[written in reminiscence during the strike]

I've walked the early morning
Orange sulphur lighted streets
With bag across my shoulder
Holding seven banded letter bundles
3 pairs of socks, and boots upon my feet.

Parcels too I've taken
Or left back by mistake
And pocketed the fivepenny fare
To buy a bun or cake
To eat before I start the round:

Door to door these houses
Back to back with outside loo
Each different with its
Brand new pseudo Oakwood door
Or its tattered brownish paint.

In most windows stands
A little tinselled Xmas tree;
Within – the average 3 piece suite
Some front rooms full
Of washing, others neat

I've walked the early morning
Puddled sulphur lighted streets
I was a "post-lady" for a week
But no postmen walk the streets now
They've taken other jobs I hear.

Sally Dalglish   Nelson, Lancs

Your Thousandth Mile   9 February 1971

I marched your thousandth mile with you
My first
You'll march but never change
The ways of laws or wars
Yet come with me and we can change
A mural into a poem
Love into cups of jasmine tea
With honey
Time into liquorice-like tobacco
And the distance between us
Into kisses

Sally Dalglish

Under The Trees   June 1971

You sweet lover under the strange familiar trees
You with me on the springy downy grass
How hopelessly we drew
Yet one in one we flew,
Green gold exploding from the Christmas tree
Below my feet.

The sun kissed our hair
All the world's love was there
Rhythms of the stream, the grasses, curlew cries
The clouds' flight never changed
But we changed
The air was sweeter, clearer with our ecstasy

But our pictures never made it
We could not snare nature on our paper
Undrawn were slopes of whortleberry, fern and firs,
Soft granite mulling in the sun
And spruces, larches, oaks
Revitalising their age-long branches

We caressed the intangible life of knowing
The ten-dimensional existence of our eyes
We crossed the transparent colours
And vibrations of life
Into the far-beyond
And tomorrow will be one day nearer
Our future.

Sally Dalglish   Wicken Clough

Apostrophe to a Young Alsation   November 1971

Oh thou great breaker of percolators!
Thou destroyer of the rubber mat, the carpet and the cacti
Distributor of washing powder, sugar, porridge oats
Thou grumbly-growling, talking-whining
Heap of uncoordinated fun
Thou art the masticator of my mail
The elusive creature of my calls
The torment of my early morning apprehensions
The subject and the master of the shoe
The gamboller on the Wasteground

You are
The coward on the run
Pursued by larger canine breeds
The playful crocodile when friends call round
The successful speculator on the Bone Exchange.
You're soft and strong as water
You're a discredit to the lupine species
For your affection
But a champion to them
In your capacity for destruction.

Sally Dalglish   Naples Street

Snow Watch   December 1971

Snow watch, slow, slow, slow watch
Timed day, timid day and
Ghastly night. Where tears go
No-one knows. Softly, softly
In your arms I breathe, waiting
Hoping for your reprieve.

Sadly wantonly I wait while
The snow flow stills on the ground
And the timed day, dark night
Recede in my imagination.
Tears fall heavenward, earthbound.
Lights in lachrymae are prismatic.

You too will yearn for forgiveness
Direction, peace and praise.
John your name will not be forgotten
With strangers who cross the sand
While waves crash on the rocks
And seagulls, double Z-shaped
Swirl in the sky of oblivion.

Sally Dalglish   Naples Street

Dam Square   August 1971

I hear the coke can clatter on the cobble square
I watch the bored and mindless faces
of all the people there
Feel the ennui of time, passing
With great emptiness, but full of care

The weary breadless youth with faces of despair
Half breathe the hash and filth that
fills the air
Here is everyone: doing nothing, going nowhere
Waiting for a minute's entertainment
Or for the men to flush and sweep the square

Here we wait for friends
And fritter away our coins
Nothing happens, each day ends
More vacuous than before.

These people slouch about
In real fab gear
Leather, suede and velvet, hats and
rings they wear
No-one has a dime
Each only worlds of time
But no imagination, little soul
No wish to move, no urge
To make a work of art, a mark

Maybe these people are free
All web-bound within
Their ego spheres
Maybe these people can love
They certainly rarely give.
The genii of the world they are
Here they sit and stand
Dreaming about some new world they've planned

So many individuals
So much hidden talent
Waiting for some-one to give them a break
While their spurious talents rot.

Sally Dalglish   Amsterdam

32.

Strangers Passing on a Train   October 1972

I want to be queen of the flowers
I want to impart the peace
That goddess gave to me.

I have suffered the beauty
of those flat Sussex fields
held among the browning autumn beeches
I swooned in the gold whitening
bracken lying by the still
acacia trees. I wept
That the reds and russets, golds and browns
The birches, rhodies, berries
Would all be intangible memory
In two hours, as I juddered
back to the bricks and dust
the lights and lifelessness of
Bustling London

Only I felt this. Only I wept
No communication
Will make my loved one feel or know what I felt
But she
With her bruised soul
So elegant with her aura wounded, melting, firm
She knew. We smiled the same smile for a second
She sat in her poised fine simplicity and welcomed
A chocolate biscuit out of a polythene bag saying, "Bread."

She said that she'd been there too
overwhelmed by the peace
surprised by the inebriating air
After our lungs had been trained to
Siphon out the smog and soot of cities.

She never said goodbye but she said
"Thank you" as she left.

Sally Dalglish   Haslemere to Waterloo

33.

Till Cobwebs Cover the Sky   1972

I offer you no chains
Nor can I be your slave
But I will cherish and caress you
Till cobwebs cover the sky
And all the trees are coal
Beneath the ground
I will cease to feel for you
When snowflakes no longer fall
And every leaf is unmoved
By the fiercest gale.
I will be gentle and tender
And talk with you
Till chapattis are no longer
Indian or Pakistani
Till the end of poetry and art
Then will we part.

Sally Dalglish   Naples Street

From the Spider's Web by Sally Dalglish

Supplication   1972

Ever present rainclouds!
Replenish my springs
With pure water
That I may flow
On my way
To the ocean
Refreshed and able
To overcome the sharpest rocks,
With strength enough to wear away
The insurmountable banks
That prevent my path
From being straight.

Sally Dalglish   Bretton Hall

Ignorance   1974

Confidence is a thing I rarely have
I do not have it when I'm alone
I have it in a crowd
I'm a very daring, extroverted person
In a crowd, even at a party
But I am not steady and resolute
With such profound comprehension
Of all the facets of living as you
This is the impression you give me
For my own good
So that I may improve
But I can feel worse and
More ignorant and more suppressed
In your company than anyone else's

Someone called last night
When you were bathing
He played your guitar
And speaking before thinking
As is my tendency I said
"Still playing madrigals?"
To which he replied by naming
The precise work of Bach he was playing
Ignorance is no defence.

Sally Dalglish   Nuttall Road

Difficulty of Getting Through   1977

I wanted to say, "Will you talk with me?"
I wanted to walk with you as a friend
But this tree stands in the way

There are no leaves on this tree
There are no birds meeting here
The boughs hang or beat about in the wind
The Cheshire cat beams aimlessly
From a branch

But you who have the power of the wind
You who could make the rain fall
The sap rise, the tree live
You stand
Somewhere behind the tree

And one day will you walk along
That path of harmony with me?
Can we look at this tree and see
Each twig dance in the wind
But not in aimless fury?

I wanted to say, "Will you talk with me?"
I wanted to walk with you as a friend
Instead I am driven to stand in your way.

Sally Dalglish   Bingley Beckfoot

May 13th Ten Years On   13 May 1981

I have thrown a pearl in the well.
No sound will recall the timbre of your voice
No embrace will replace your frame.
Wracked with dismissing
All that gave me joy
And delightful pain
I hover doubtfully eying
Spring with indifference
Cooking for no-one in particular
Polishing for no purpose
Since you're gone.

Sally Dalglish   John Peel Cottage

38.

Fleeced by Night   1982

Shepherd cloaked by night
Keep warm the weary weaver by your side
Dog howls.   Breeze slips
Through your black felt tent
And the ewes murmur
Goats droopy-eared stand silently

Wool your world, guls the highlight of your life
Rams' horns adorn your rugs and bags
Complement your life

Shepherd cloaked by night
You do not stir
When three strangers cross the hill
Seven times they come
And seven times again
And seven more
And once – for fortune's sake
They come before your door

In slumber you hear them not
And do not hear the first
Who turns wood into fire
Wood he has brought from afar
To the fire he adds the droppings he has gathered
The second uses the light the first has made
Tobacco he brings to while away the time

The third gets out his pipe and plays three songs
The first is glad, the second sad, the third a lullaby
Light, time and music for ever changing, for ever
Present, flit in their seven ways

As the weaver sleeps she sees the candle flames
The heads of the sheep as the trusting follow on
She sees the shadow and its sun
And in between: the goat whose hair, smooth shaft,
She mingles with the staple to be spun

Seven and herself will spin: enough wool
For the weaver's rug
Year by year as they wander they watch the madder grow
Root dug in eighth year will make the finest dye
Token of blood of every living creature
So closely woven into the texture of creation

Shepherd cloaked by night
What tales you will tell tomorrow
As you water the flock
Not knowing that three strangers came in the night

Weaving woman as you stir your grapeleaf vats
And dry your yarns for eight hours in the sun
In sleep you heard the flautist blow
In your rug you'll weave his harmony and patterns
But you did not know
Three strangers came in the night.

Sally Dalglish   Weaver's Cottage Graffham

Perspective   1982

The least insect on the mirror
Is more important than I
Minute as he is he can preen
He can dance, be still and fly
He's at one with his maker
Trusting, astute
He's sublime – a fakir
Beautiful, sans toute:
Toutes les choses que les hommes
Desirent, travaillent, souffrient.

Ah! Sweet iridescent angel
Dancing on my arm
Black as night
Performing your ablutions
On my wrist
Each hand hair of mine
You have kissed
Sweet tiny angel
Vaster than I by far
In your obedience to the Maker's will
I shall return again
To your state.

Sally Dalglish   Heyshott, Sussex

The Place Where I Live   1982

In the stillness in the greenhouse in the petals of a flower
In the vacuum in the man-made heating grill
In the ceaseless flickering ferns
        sensitive to less than breeze
In the quarter jug of milk gone sour
In the crumbling paintwork on the bathroom windowsill
In each hedgehog quill and parasite: there live I.

In the stillness of the colour of the fragrance
        of a flower: there live I
In the stagnant backwater, as a tadpole:
        there live I
In the beauty of the throbbing heart of all:
        there live I.

Sally Dalglish   Selham, West Sussex

Praise for the Grey Days 1982

Thank you Great Spirit of Life for your mercies
Thank you for the leafless trees and the rain
Thank you for the deep dark times in my mind
The cloaking grey awaiting the moment of sun

Rest moody alive we are but sleeping
Grey beings enhanced by perennial birdsong
Swaying, buffeted by the winds, we know
Your heart-life is in all, through all and beyond all.

Sally Dalglish   Graffham

Folkestone   10 July 1983

Gravely we walk the streets above
Gingerly we descend the slope
But on the beach we shout with love
We dance and dash and dot the sand
Daring the sea foam
With screams of glee and smiles of hope
We bounce the ball and sift the sand
For signs of life uncommon in our daily world.
Abandon trammels all who enter here
One sanded foot is all we need to cheer.

Sally Dalglish

Souvenir [for an Oxford-bound medical student]   7 August 1983

The moment after you are gone
Is bare
No rug on the grass brings you back
Gone are your bare black feet
Your hair
That Adonis look you wear
And gone too – no, not quite gone
Is the unique timbre of your voice
The incisive look of your compassionate eye
Aye, but the rift; when yesterday
You were – just another introduction
In front of whom I poured out
My unchecked complaint
About silent living, weather
Tedium – and you, amused
Let all these comments slip you by.

In the garden summer sun
Each caress dotted the pool of my affection
With soothing ripples
Balmy the breath that beat
Refreshment on my brow
Sweet drums you played on hip skin hollow
And bites! What teeth!
Why! How you thrummed my vertebrae
Dispersing tensions at a touch. But only the physical
presence
And the sounds have I lost

All else exists formless
Not in a form of might-have-been
Traces of you are stamped on every aspect
Of now...each moment...

The moments after the moment after you're gone
Are full
Of peacefulness, confidence and calm
Your rug in the boot, your souvenir
Of wool and goats' hair
Some young Afshari maiden's work of art
Gift to the man she vows to cherish
I give to you – for a sum
Only because you liked it
It will look well in the violin shop
Unique artefact with rosy aura
Easy to overlook – so simple and crude
If compared with more classic rugs

I saw your sadness as you backed away
Only the subtle deeper shades of indigo
Only the blues make the rose madder
Look so divinely tongue-like warm
Kiss me – Tom – sweet, yes, what a souvenir!

La tristesse seulement me montre
Que tu veut revenir a moi.
Ah! The memory, the memory.

Sally Dalglish   Graffham

My Tabernacle   9 August 1983

My tabernacle
Was an ice altar
That I built
In the sloping snowfield
Between Manor Farm and Heyshott
I was ten
It remained
Several days
After the snow was gone.

Sally Dalglish

Braithwaite Moss   21 March 1984

So shall she see over a stile
Water as bright and well-directed as this?
Flickering dead fireweed across the ribbonned flow
And there a split-ringed stump
Etched in umber cracks, cream beige lines and chocolate.

Pad on the moss – rush valley bed
Pad by the easy-time water channel
Of fine water. Inviting territory
Welcoming dog – no, not so biddable collie
Of a couple sitting in a tree.

Sally Dalgish   Cumbria

Collar Dove   1985

I am
The dove
The collar dove
You sought

Stronger
Than all other
Scavenging birds

Chase away the
Dark Rooks
Of your thought
I will

And eat the food
And splash in the bird bath water
You left
For other
Lesser birds

I fly
And cheat and lie
And
Like the others love and live and die

But you sought
A holy white messenger
An emblem of peace

And stood resolute
Unswerving
Aiming your gun
At all impostors

But there are
Too many of us
Mightier and more suburban
Than the feral pigeon

We are

We are
So numerous
And breed and coo
Unceasingly

And our message
Is not peace
Or strife
Or greed
Or just ascendancy
It is the collar dove
Who wears the mark
Yoked to divinity
This messenger
Surveys the territory
And cries:
O! Live!

Sally Dalglish					Warwick Square

The Doormat   12 June 1983

I am the mat upon which
Many a feline fella hath sat
Not Tom, but many a
Cool clever cat

I am the magic placid mat
Who takes away your dross

I sit at the threshold
Of your refuge
And everyone who passes
Wipes his feet and leaves
The residue of his understanding:
Baked clay and dust
Which for me with
Ethereal air and water
Spell life

Mat of camel hue am I
Woven of coconut fibre
The nut milk drunk
Thirst quenched
Flesh eaten. . . .

He was a way, a door
A light, a path
But I [unlike the mighty greats]
Am quite content to lie

At the feet of all
And serve quite passively
Collecting the bits that people
Leave behind, leaving them free
To lay aside their travels
And in what they leave
I conjure up a universe.

Sally Dalglish   Graffham

The Note Under the Mat   1985

Underneath the baked clay
From which Man will be made
Lies the mat of camel hue
Woven of coconut fibre
Milkless nut coat.

Underneath the mat
Lies a recess in the stone
So that no-one
Will trip from a raised mat.
A mat raised above
The wonderful mosaic plan
Of mankind – the endless floor –
Would be of no benefit
Would merely make stumble
Every guest into this world.

Underneath the recess
Lies the foundation
Granite depths
The surety of Law.

But underneath the granite
Lies the earth
Teeming with dark-loving creatures
And below that, clay.
More mankind possibly
Or something else.

And underneath the clay
Is the water
Of moving, living, irrepressible Truth
Wending its way in accordance
With gravity
Seeking the sunshine and sea,
The open air.

And underneath the waterways
What interminable depths
Of countless substances!
Who can core the earth?

And deep within
The vast volcanic
Sulphuric, brimstone and ash-making
Potential: the mighty fire force
Impenetrable:
Hidden co-respondent of the sun
Phoenix – the ashes are almost cold
Way down, underneath the mat.

Sally Dalglish   Warwick Square

A Change on the Face of Mistress Earth   1984

I know he cares
He touches me
With raindrop fingers
Caressing the receptive earth
Strokes like the
Pockets of wind
Upon which every bird flies
Kindles the loving candlelight
In my bones
Such a gentle transformation
Was not to be expected.

Sally Dalglish

Not So Lucky   19 January 1991

She was an oasis of affection in an arid world
My courtesan for tickles, touches, strokes of
passion, belly rubs and purrs
And as I kissed the blood in the bowl
Where she had lain
I felt the racy, sweet saltness
Of her daredevil existence: no tree or roof unclimbed
No cupboard left uninvestigated
No warm chair by the fire
Had not been curled up in by her
Personal conversation
Always superceded
Food
Imprinted in my mind are
Countless uncurling stretches
Tail high, bottom pertly raised
And front paws grasping the furthest inch
Of carpet.
Oh starry eyes where are you now?
Plaintive mewer behind a door
You have gone through the final door
In your endless black cat dashes
Across the road
"Dear Lucky!" we wept, "Dearest
Wonderful cat," we gently sobbed
As we buried that pile of rags
Beneath the blackest of red roses.

Little soul beloved more than any other
We see her everywhere:
She has painted every room
With her spirit of curiosity and repose.
I keep falling into a stupour of calm
Mistaking it for serenity

There was nothing to forgive in Lucky
She was full of delight, beautiful and faultless
An angel in bib and booties
Impossible to conceive the abolition
Of such intelligence, feline grace
Such sweet affection and appeal

Gone is my darling:
In perfect health, coat combed
Eyes cleaned, fastidiously fed
Now dead.
Only mortality
Swipes at the heart
And removes the priceless beloved
In a moment..

Just a little walk at twilight
To accompany a guest
Reversing out of the drive
Onto a double bend.

His sudden change of direction
Caught Lucky unawares
As she darted and was transfixed
On the double lines.

A friend said, "Savour the moments of calm.
Lucky came for a reason and you've
Shared many experiences.
She has given you great insight.

"Dearest Lucky!" we wept. "Dearest
Wonderful cat," we gently sobbed
As we buried that pile of rags
Beneath the blackest of red roses.

Sally Dalglish   Brackenwell

O Fishes!   1992

O Fishes! The pool in which I stand
And thrash about, breaking the images
Of your sun and moon is sometimes still
As I gaze at the splendour of their reflections.

Sally Dalglish   Roseberry Road

Tranquillity

1 July 2001

And as the sun rests
On the pattering sea edge
And the breeze lifts
There is a peaceful place
There am I

Sally Dalglish

Gargrave

Yena Couja!   23 November 1997

Seeing you and speaking with you
Is like being with your boyhood
By some familiar trees, barefoot
Ready to run and laugh and tumble
As if at twelve we knew not
Any of the tattered ribbons
The sad heartaches, the endless toil.

Each time I hear your voice
In me stirs a fresh new brook, a spring
And I pass the hours while you strive
In idle longing dreams and prepare
Only a comfortable coal fire
A small spot where you might rest
For an hour...

Yes the rhinoceros comes in white leather
To my taunts of "Pachydermis!"
He may seem thick-skinned but
He is ultra-sensitive and so are you.
But can I get one arrow to pierce your hide
So that you will circle and then charge me?
"Yena couja! Yena couja! He is coming."

Sally Dalglish   Carlisle

The Lotus Flower   2 August 2002

Time with you
Is like time watching
A lotus flower unfold
In its deep pool:
One petal, then another
And a complete pause in between

And so unfolds another perfect form
In this dance of a thousand petals:
Each soft caress
Of hand on hair
Lip on temple
Finger on breast

The fullness of the first gaze
And touch becomes more glorious
As the lotus blossom
Exquisitely slowly
Releases itself.

Sally Dalglish   Stanwix

The Lotus Flowers by Sally Dalglish

What Do I Now Believe? 27 January 2000

Communion for me is when eyes meet
Not crispbread and vinegar
Belief for me is not the mumbo-jumbo
Of mytharised baloney called a Creed
It is this:
I am here now
I do not know
Anything
For sure
All I possess
Is some trace memory
Of my experiences
Subject to varying interpretations
And in my life there is a trinity:
A situation exists – fleetingly.
It is revealed by a light thrown onto it.
A shadow is cast.

I live most of my life
In that shadow.

By the great exertion
Of willpower
And ceaseless manoeuvring
Of my hand of cards
I may engineer myself
Into that rainbow of light
And travel easily to

My destination.
I may reach the light before death or after.
The light exists.

Sally Dalglish											Samye Ling

Blaeberry Fell

13 January 2002

I carried my Japanese wrestler
In my mind along Blaeberry Fell
I felt the force of the dancing bear
In the hundred foot fall at Cat Gill
Felt his subtlety
As the last autumn leaf
Grazed my cheek
Felt again his gentle touch
As a fern brushed my sleeve.
I carried my Japanese wrestler
In my mind along Blaeberry Fell.
I felt him there
With me
In my heart.

Sally Dalglish

Old Man Oak 3 October 2002

There! was the young oak tree
Festooned in the autumn sunshine.
How like Les I smiled:
The branches nibbled by
The Caldbeck ponies in the winter
Fighting back with myriad twigs
New leaves small and shrivelled
With mildew. But lots more buds.
How often have I heard him say:
"When you're knocked down
Pick yourself up and fight back."

Aggression even in the site of his ashes.

I paused for stillness
Feeling his essence surround me
And the tree that he was growing.

"I haven't forgotten you.
I still hope to carry out your plans
If you will help," I spoke aloud.

At that moment I almost heard
Him quoting Portia with:
"The quality of mercy is not strained
It droppeth as the gentle rain from heaven
Upon the place beneath."
Raindrops fell through the sunlight
And looking North I saw the rainbow.

Sally Dalglish					Caldbeck

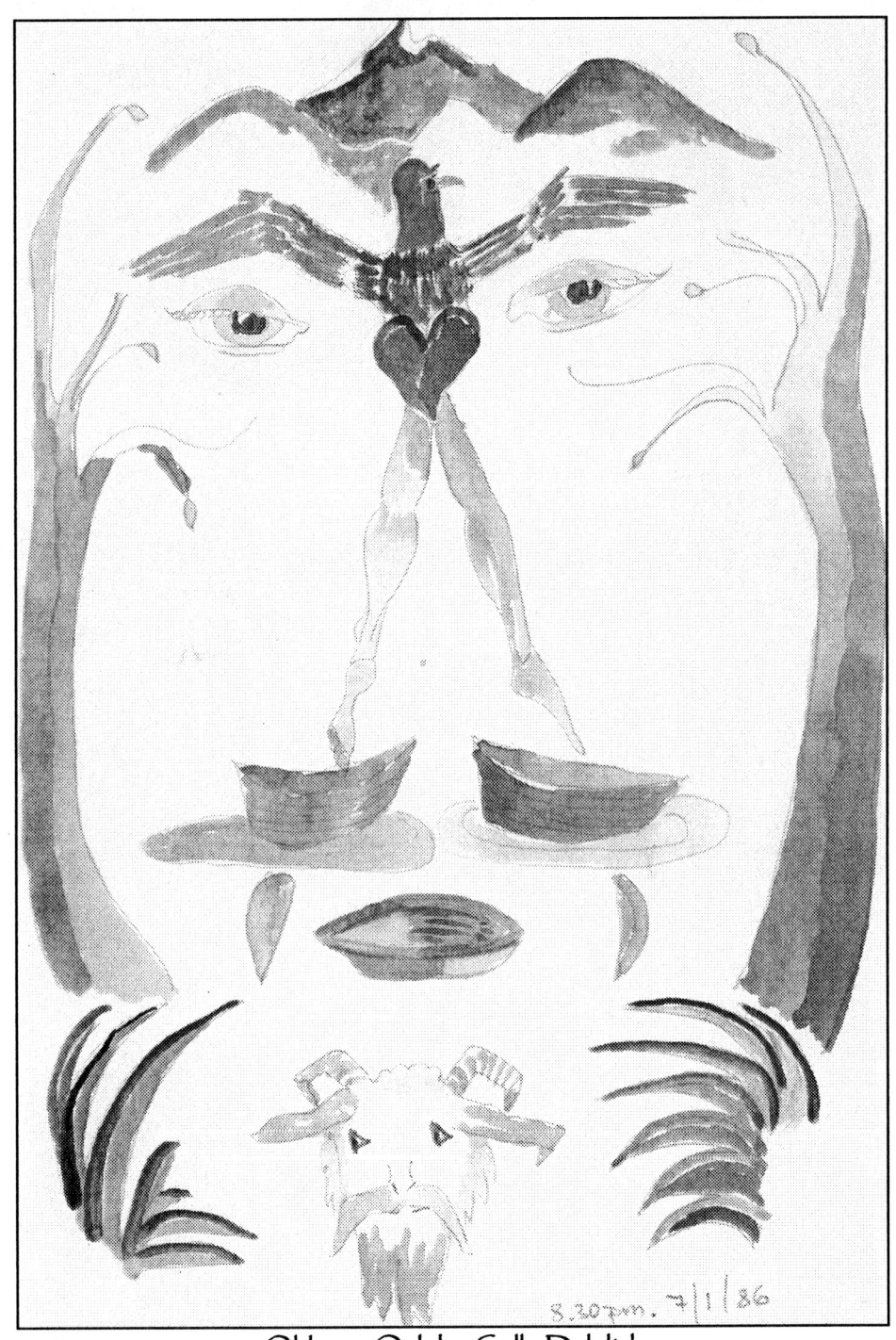

Old man Oak by Sally Dalglish

Water in a Fly's Eye

15 November 2002

I am a fly's eye in the filth
This is my life
Touch the muck and I fly
To a place to place my
Tasting feet

I rest on the meniscus
Of the dirty trickle
These girls are collecting
For their drink. Oh die!

I can sustain a life
As a fly's eye but
I cannot give relief
To my relations: these creatures
These little children
With human eyes
And souls.

Sally Dalglish   Peony House

Waller Brook, Dartmoor 1957   8th May 2003

Waller Brook how you weave and dart
Over small granite pebbles and tree roots
To our beloved pool,
Damned up carefully by our small fingers
With rocks and turves.
Beside us, as my brother Alex and I play
And splash
The wafting leather toasted nectar gorse
Comforts us with sun-filled fragrance.
The lumpy moss tussocks
Make a soft landing for our games.

Waller Brook! On you trickle and sing
On to the Dart and the cliffs above.
We tickle trout in the small pocket pools
But in the Dart we are taught to catch fish with a fly.
Here in our Waller Brook pool
Naked we catch each other
And cool ourselves out of the sun
In these pebbly waters.

Sally Dalglish   Mungrisedale

Water is my God   19th March 2003

Water is my God in its all and nothingness
This matrix of all living things is the
bearer of wisdom
The instrument of cosmic forces
The reflector and receiver of all sounds, moods and
impressions.
Great healer and distributor of nutrients,
At the mercy of man's freewill and his abuse,
How I daily cherish your purity and subtlety,
longing for
Nothing more than your unsullied existence!

Even motor cars will run on water
if you zap the hydrogen
And release the oxygen into the air.
Maybe they will blow up all the oil wells
in the world
And I shall not be alone in cherishing
the sacred water.

Sally Dalglish   Cumbria

End of the Rainbow   21st March 2003

WE are a death-loving culture
The sort of bacteria that thrives
Or wearily trudges through
Radiated, mechanically-produced
Technologically-inspired food
We are deadly inspired by our
News media, slurping up bowls
Of disaster, division, mortification
And disgust, sauced with death.

We deaden the water if possible
With a strangulation of economies.
We are dead as Midas,
Wanting everything to be gold
And comfortable and progressive.

People were aeons wiser before the big rat
"Progress" appeared.
We have progressed so far
Through mechanical, technological
Brilliance
That we have reached the other end
Of the rainbow
And there is no pot of gold there either
Only the mouth of a Delphic spring
Glinting in the sunlight, whispering:
"Poison me too you bastards."

Sally Dalglish   Holme Hyssop Well

62.

Tearing the Ocean down   24th March 2003

As I, a teardrop, gaze at you and
Your unending waving, ocean,
You are part of me,
As a teardrop

All I seek
Is a reflection of beauty
For I am unsullied,
As a teardrop.

But you
You cannot resist
The temptation
To desecrate and destroy
Because your resistance
Is not yet grown.
Oh waving ocean!
You are a childish breaker
An ignorant despoiler
Waiting for revelation,
Peace, comfort, stability
To reign.

Sally Dalglish

Heretical Fish

28th March 2003

Christianity is a net
Pitted with holes.
Tiddlers like you and me
Can swim through free
Into the Universal Deep
But the full-grown Christians
Get stuck in the net
And raised up to the Kingdom of Heaven
Weighed, sold and eaten.

Sally Dalglish   Carlisle

Heretical Fish by Sally Dalglish

The Source   25 December 2003

My impulse was to go to Midnight Mass
On Wigton Road and be part of the emotion,
The special Celebration
But I'm so against the Creed.
I do believe she had a human partner
But was good at keeping secrets.
There are so many parts of the myth
With which I cannot reconcile myself
That I thought instead
"I'll go down to Hyssop Holme well,
My dear source of excelling water
And bless its purity, modesty and
Clean, refreshing holiness.

I go there at Christmas because
It is a chilly, fireless place
That no-one wants, at Christmas.

Sally Dalglish

The Water Garden

Section II

Water Aid

1.

Sahelian Earth

This season is for baobabs
Baobabs are princes of height.
Their swollen feet command
A whole empire under earth

        Above the baobabs,
        Seagulls dive in and out of brackish waters.
        They stare at us with country-bred eyes.
        They stare at us like Serere fishermen from Joal

The sun radiates above splinter boughs.
This is a season of desolate laughters.
Very little water has fallen
To comfort our souls.
Very little water has fallen
On palmfronds to support
The throats of crows.

Rains have signed a contract of neglect
With our landscape. Rains have signed a contract of neglect.
Our soils are bare, without grass or shrubs,
Without weeds or creepers. Our inheritance
Has suddenly turned into
The restless despair of the camel's fate.
Only the baobabs stride majestically
In our landscape; their octopus branches
Cling to some ancient hope.

        We sweat till our bodies shrivel like bonga fish.
        We sweat to cool off our body fires.
        Sweat is catharsis for us.
        God pours down cold water from the inside.

We build bamboo houses to recuperate
Our laughter from the anguish of the sun.
We build earthen wells to welcome God's recharge
Of our silent aquifers.

        We do not have the patience of baobabs.
        We do not have their appetites for storing water.
        So God pour down your rain more often.
        Pour garlands of water in our claypots and jars.

For water is sap, sustenance to our ailing laughter.
Water is peat, manure to sprouting seedlings.
Water is germ-root, river to the vitality of our hearts.
Water is hope, roads of promise to our fisherman's yearnings.
Water is the baptismal pool, livestock drift to it
To slake their thirst.
Water is dreams, restoring glitter
To the future of our farms.
Water is the gem-rock of Dusty Kingdoms.

Tijan M. Sallah

Picture Yourself

Picture yourself in a Third World place,
And see the look on a villager's face,
Who has just found out that their only daughter,
Has died through drinking a glass of water.
Now put yourself in their position,
Your daughter has died, young, full of ambition;
We take water for granted: it's always there,
Some people don't think, others don't care.
Now picture yourself in a Third World place.
I'm sure you'll think twice about the water you waste.

Adam Barratt, age 13, St Pauls Roman Catholic Secondary School, Leicester.

The Little Girl at the Tap   15 January 2003

It isn't her little brown eyes
that draw her to me
nor her oversized dress.

it isn't her shy expression
it must be something more.

The tap stand seems out of reach
she's standing on tip toe.
I sense her anticipation
she craves to take that drink.

The water comes out slowly
trickling down her face
diluting a smudge
it flows down with grace.
She cups her hands and drinks.

Her eyes shine and sparkle
she shyly smiles at me.
Thanking me without a word
Saying so much more.

It was the first tap stand
near the village school,
the second is two miles on.

It isn't her little brown eyes
nor her oversized dress
but the hope she inspires me.

Enid Katorobo

4.

Sweet, sweet Water   5 March 1996

Sweet sweet water
cover me
wash away my misery.

Hug me
Warm me
Cradle me
So I can swim
In thee with glee.

Sweet sweet water
cover me
wash away my misery.

Fears that taunt me
Tease me
Haunt me
Thoughts assailing:
Shower them clean.

Sweet sweet water
cradle me
wash away my misery.

Enid Katorobo

5.

If   15 January 2003

If
i had buckets of water
that could never run out

If i could splash them on Africa
that could clear some doubt

If
i were more than a dreamer
that could work more than shout

I would open up streams
in deserts of hope
then dry the tears if you cry

I have two pennies in a bucket
i've dollars and a pound
that should do for now.

Enid Katorobo

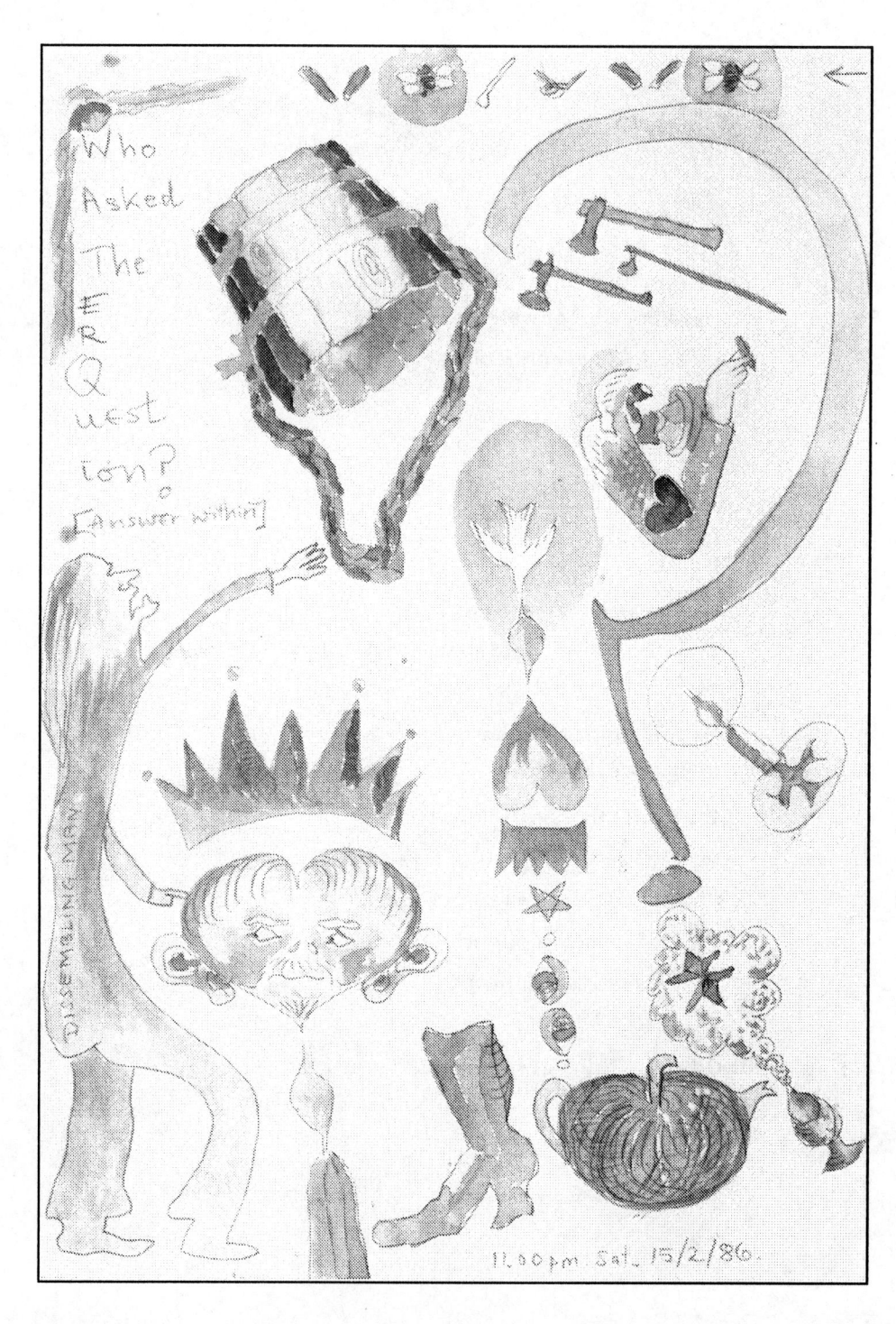

A Bucket of Dreams by Sally Dalglish

6.

Water! – A plea for those without

Do you want diamonds
that glitter so bright
Or fireworks that dazzle
and light up the night?

How about 'planes that
Will take you to Mars?
Or rockets that orbit
The moon and the stars?

Would you like money –
coins of silver and gold?
Or hats, scarves and mittens
to keep out the cold?

Do you want TV – cable or sky
CD's and videos – expensive to buy?
Big houses with garages – red brick or stone
A porsche, a caravan, a new mobile phone?

Game boys, computers
Would you ask for such things?
Bracelets and watches
and beautiful rings?

Maybe a bedroom
packed full of toys?
Poke'mon figures
for girls and for boys?

Harry Potter Broomsticks
and wands for your spells?
With Ron, Hermione
and Hagrid as well?

But are <u>these</u> important
Is that what you think?
All I need is fresh water
Quite simply – a drink.

Written by class 9 of Horton Grange First School in Blyth. The children are 8-9 year olds and have been raising money for WaterAid over the last year by donating 5p of their swimming money change each week.

Water Can Be

I can fall from a cloud in the sky
I can run down a cheek from an eye
I can be in the river and see all the fishes,
or wash people's pots and glasses and dishes
I can be sea and covered with boats,
If it wasn't for me they couldn't float.
I quench people's thirst and taste really nice,
and if I am frozen I am then called ice.
I can be boiled and then I'm called steam,
or frozen and eaten and then I'm ice cream.
I'm called Hydrogen Oxide, but my nickname is shorter,
If you don't know by now, I'd best tell you – I'm water!

By Gareth Wilson, aged 15. Leesbrook Community Sports College, Derby.

Oh No! It's Raining Again

Oh no it's raining again will it never stop,
Falling from the sky in great big drops

Forming giant puddles stopping me going out
Wait, hurray is that the sun coming out?

Mixing with raindrops there forms a rainbow
The farmers will be glad the crops will grow

It's strange as we watch the raindrops fall
To think that some have no water at all

There the ground is dusty, hard and dry
If they do not drink they will surely die

So when we moan the weather's bad
We really should not be so sad

Because children who are far away
Would love to see a rainy day.

Benjamin Hopwood, age 8   Vernon Lodge School

9.

The Umbrella Seller

The old men sit in the village square
Smoking their pipes in the noonday sun.
They dwell upon the lack of rain
Discuss the damage being done.

They look up to a cloudless sky
Past the trees with withered leaves
Past the whitewashed buildings where
The window boxes hold no dreams

A breeze blows in. Net curtains caught
In disbelief grasp it and weave
Slow motion flimsy images:
'Like clouds collecting' old Juan thought

'The harvest will be poor this year'
'Young Pedro lost two cows last week'
'My vineyard is a winter's tale.
God knows what we are going to do'

Their brooding stops. They've heard the bus
Ramshackle down the dusty street
It stops outside the small hotel
A dog barks. Hens investigate

A weary passenger alights
The journey's taken her four days.
But now she stands where Caesar stood
(Or near to where he passed this place)

She's studying history (Caesar's wars)
Where Roman armies marched she goes
Charting ancient history trails,
Mapping an empire's glorious reign.

She dreams of water, cold as ice
Clean clothes, a coffee (make it black)
A shower or two to wash away
The grit and grime of travelling.

Outside the hotel in the booth
Where old Maria once sold flowers
An umbrella seller sits
Surrounded by his rainbow colours

She looks at him. He winks at her
She smiles but inwardly sighs
'God knows what I'm going to do
If it should rain while I am here'.

Terry Marston, a WaterAid Supporter in Australia

Delayed by Rough Seas

The Celtic, pilgrim, sailor saints
set out to find the promised land
in open boats
of skins stretched out on wood:
the Cross and just themselves
was all they carried.
Carrying within their hearts
the God they sought;
exiles for the love of Christ,
they hoped to reach their true home.
Mystics, no longer longing for
that unattainable other world
mythical island, Land of Promise, hidden
beyond the vastness of the sea.
Speaking the universal language
of Christ's love,
birds, all nature, joining
in their psalms and chanting,
singing praise to their creator God.
Hunger and thirst they knew,
knowing heaven's fullness.
Their sails full set and flying
through the sacramental sea,
or becalmed and drifting,
shipping oars and trusting
to the providence of God.
Sailing by the stars,
encountering demons,

storms without, within;
what was important was the journey,
delayed by God to teach them secrets
of the ocean, their inner lives.

Fearless they braved the angry sea
but still they feared the final journey
we all must travel to God's presence,
into the dark unknown, alone.

David Hodges, a monk of the Cistercian Abbey on Caldey Island off the south coast of Wales.

11.

The Sea, The Sea

'Beware of the Sea!
If thou hearest the cry of the gull on the shore
Thy heart shall then rest in the forest no more.

JRR Tolkien, "The Lord of the Rings"

Who would live
far from the sound of water and the gull,
from boats and ropes,
the smell of the sea
and the salt air?
To be at one
with the ocean's sigh,
the breakers and the spray.

Who would live
and not be wakened
by the lap of water
on the shore,
by the sound of the tide
pouring back through shingle,
by the cry of the gulls
riding the sky,
and the creak of wooden boats?

Who would live
and not be entranced
by young seals
basking on the rocks,
by peregrines
hunting the cliffs,
by the sparkle of the sulight
on clear water,
or the tide come racing in
like lace upon the shore?

Who would live
and not be enthralled
by the sight of white tops,
by the lashing of the ocean waves,
or the sound of the surf
booming in the sea caves
and come crashing in
upon the wild and rocky shore?

And then at nightfall,
be at one
with the stillness,
black and deep,
with the calming rhythm
of the tranquil sea,
a pool of silver
in the moonlight.

David Hodges

We Came from the Sea by Sally Dalglish

Nature Notes

Sunrise, the ritual moment
the ancient archetypal play
enacts; the pure event,
when dark gives way to light.
Gulls dance and golden water
laps the crystal sand.
The soul shivers; the day breaks
like sacred music
arising from the depths of being.
The indescribable reverence
of early morning sounds,
the hesitant cry of the first bird
now taken up by others,
as the tidal landscape
replaces the dark and silence
of the still retreating night.
The stars give way, the cosmos
attunes to a new day.

David Hodges

Pilgrimage

Sharing space
in the wild
with a gnarled
black walnut tree,
born out of the landscape,
in the endless
empty plain.
I am glad
of its deep shade
and of the water-hole
shimmering
beneath the burning heat,
where dreams surface,
self is encountered,
and illusions shattered;
where wounds are healed,
and reality faced,
where God is tasted,
in the slow
march of time,
on the path of longing,
towards that holy place
we travel to.

David Hodges

Wilderness

Wilderness weather,
a lull in the
unforgiving
horizontal rain.
The seascape boundless,
rugged headland
after rugged headland,
the peregrine hunting,
gulls riding the wind.
The soul stiff with cold.
Dusk comes quickly.

David Hodges

15.

A Winter Sunset

A red gel orb,
fiery liquid
dripping red,
sinks beneath
a sea of angry blue.
The red sun slides
below the ocean's rim,
pulsing light
and fire on water.
And in the afterglow
of bright refracted light,
appear uncharted oceans
set with islands
in the sky.
I seem to sense
some strange
new other world
that draws me there,
that touches
deep within,
felt somehow
through distances
that seem so near
yet far,
on some other shore
the other side
of silence .

David Hodges

The Playfulness of God

Out of a milky sea,
huge white-topped rollers
poised to crash,
pounding against red rock,
the foam pushed high,
hung in suspense
like a freeze-frame,
floating on air, then
pouring up ragged cliffs,
spume flecking,
driven by a wild wind
across undulating fields
of bent grass.

A flock of starlings,
together rising,
cheeky stunt fliers
challenging the gusting wind,
all in formation,
then circling and pirouetting,
disappearing, reappearing,
a trick of the light,
an aerial ballet, then
playfully tossing like acrobats
over a drystone wall,
scattering on the meadow
like fallen leaves.

In the playfulness of God,
all is now and wonder.

David Hodges

Birds Migrating South

That unearthly silence,
that moment suspended in time,
before the rise
with the flutter of many wings
and muffled cries,
circle, peel off, loop and cross,
join,
divide again.
Birds in formation,
nearer, further,
nearer, further,
as they pass
and repass overhead;
suddenly
veering south,
the sight
and the sound
of a thousand
beating wings
flying seaward,
silver in the sun.

David Hodges

Rock Pool

Tranquil,
seaweed-sided,
tidal pool
with green and red
and purple fronds;
tiny fish,
black and silver,
darting in the sunlight;
microcosm
of the roaring,
rolling sea.

Absorbed
in a world
in miniature,
the mind relaxes,
worries disappear.

The rock pool
is lazy, calm,
a mirror
of the conscious mind;
the unconscious,
the thundering deep
behind.

David Hodges

Rock Pool by Sally Dalglish

19.

Nothing in November

Nothing in November
but dark days
of black seas raging,
pounding the broken shore,
blinding spray
and the foam roaring,
pouring
through the red teeth
of the red raw rock,
scarred by the buffeting
of endless storms
and the wild sea lashing.
Dark days merge into nights
when the sea of my heart
refuses rest.

When the biting cold
chills the bone,
and the endless
roar and motion,
and the cry
of the storm-tossed gulls
singing, ringing in the air;
when the howl
of the salt-laden wind,
sharp as a knife,
cuts into the soul,
until the unbearable

     endless night
    meets the dawn
    and the gentle rain.

David Hodges

The Mystic Path

Golden sun,
the air ethereal,
liquid gold the water.
It was at the end of such a day,
walking in two worlds,
belonging to none,
I thought
I could
step out along the golden highway
of the sea,
step across clouds
and reach the sun.

David Hodges

Water Aid
(The Charity)

Brilliant exercise
in lateral thinking;
India's untouchables,
below the lowest caste,
restoring precious water.
Hand-picked and trained,
to mend once idle
broken water pumps.
Breaking down
ancient barriers
with bicycles and spanners.
Despised, rejected,
now respected
in every village.
Allowed to touch
what before
they could not touch;
allowed to share
the common cup.

David Hodges

22.

Water for All – who cares?

What's she doing?
Just standing in the rain?
She must be mad,
She'll be soaked,
Just standing in the rain.

Are you alright, love?
Just standing in the rain?
I'm not mad.
I'm just being soaked,
Just standing in the rain.

I remember the sun.
Just standing in the sky.
Day after month
After year.
Soaking the withered earth
Just scorching in the heat.

You must miss the sun.
All my crops died.
You must be mad.
Then my man died.
To come to this soaking land.
Then my child died.

There was nothing I could do.
I was just standing dust.

I thought I was mad.
Soaking in despair.
Just standing in the heat.

What did I do?
I left that dying place.
No, I'm not mad.
I'm soaking in the wetness,
Crying with the rain.

Zena Haggar. Winning poem from H2003 organised by the Department for International Development of the International Year of Freshwater.

The Water Garden

SECTION III

Friends and Guides

Seeded Universe

Where you are not
I am not
Where you are
I see
Love's seeded universe

All faith
All hope
All charity
Is in you
My own tomorrow

Les Marchant 1906-2000, dear friend and guide

2.

The Wave

You and I one day will plunge into
A wave of rich remembering
That sucks us soft deep down into
A sapphire world on turquoise wings
You and I one day with Soul's caress
Shall surrender to our great Oneness
With sighs and cries we'll ride that wave
With smiling eyes, with dolphins play,
Rising falling, trough and crest
Espy the Sun sink in the West
As solar devas spin and shine
An image of a path divine
An eternity of ecstasies
Like native girls on sunny quays
Who wave their wands and sway and sing
Welcoming us home again
To islands in a crystal sea
That never has forsaken we
Who gleam like jewels in Arcady
Set in our memory's shimmering lea
Where crimson flowers unfold with bliss
Like parting lips, a galactic kiss
Swallows us whole into a place
Where there's no borderline or race
Where there's no need to prove or try
No fears to make us live a lie
No blood that bleeds, no hearts that ache
No drink to drown or drugs to fake

Exquisite feelings that the State
Has disallowed because they break
The spell that they cast over us
The amnesia that removed the trust
Contaminated love with lust.
For now those longings long denied
Have swelled into the turning tide
The very wave that now is surging
The Great Tsunami now returning
Bearing all the truth and blessings
That ever played upon our heartstrings.
So let our singing sun-heart be
Allowing all our eyes to see
Allowing all our love to free
The golden bird that's caged within
The illusions of our pain and sin
Those veils that tranquillised the wrench
When plundered was our innocence
By forces hard that had no sense
Of the melodies we came to make
Of the wonder that we incarnate
Like swallows drawn to foreign climes
As travellers borne from other times
We have arrived at last to claim
The birthright of our Spirit's aim:
Compassion for all living things
As we crawl or fly or run or swim
The rocks and rivers, flowers and trees
All sacred now shall all life be
A cosmic dance and symphony
Conducted by Humanity

Lyn Birkbeck, astrologer and guide

3.

Mathnawi [I,3555-8]   Jelaluddin Rumi [1207-1273]
From **Rumi Daylight – A Daybook of spiritual Guidance**

The Prophet said, "When you lay one finger
over an eye, you see the world without the sun.
One fingertip hides the moon –
and this is a symbol of God's covering –
the whole world may be hidden from view
by a single point,
and the sun may be eclipsed by a splinter."
Close your lips and gaze on the sea within you:
God made the sea subject to man.

4.

Mathnawi [II, 566-8]   Jelaluddin Rumi [1207 – 1273]
From Rumi Daylight – A Daybook of Spiritual Guidance

The reflection cast from good friends is needed
until you become, without the aid of any reflector,
    a drawer of water from the Sea.
Know that the reflection is just an imitation,
    but when it continues to recur,
    it turns into direct realisation of truth.
Until it has become realisation,
don't part from the friends who guide you –
    don't break away from the shell
if the raindrop hasn't yet become a pearl.

5.

Mathnawi [II, 716-8]   Jelaluddin Rumi [1207 – 1273]
From Rumi Daylight – A daybook of Spiritual Guidance

The beauty of the heart
is the lasting beauty:
its lips give to drink of the water of life.
Truly it is the water, that which pours,
and the one who drinks – all three
become one when your talisman is shattered.
That oneness you can't know by reasoning

6.

Mathnawi [II, 1020-1]   Jelaluddin Rumi [1207 – 1273]
From Rumi Daylight – A Daybook of Spiritual Guidance

    Know that the outward form passes away,
    but the world of reality remains for ever.
    How long will you play at loving the shape of the jug?
    Leave the jug; go, seek the water!

7.

Mathnawi [II, 3296-3302]   Jelaluddin Rumi [1207 – 1273]
From **Rumi Daylight: A Daybook of Spiritual Guidance.**

The surface of thought's stream
carries sticks and straws –
some pleasant, some unsightly.
Seed-husks floating in the water
have fallen from fruits of the invisible garden.
Look for the kernels back in the garden,
for the water comes from the garden into the riverbed.
If you don't see the flow of the water of Life,
Look at this movement of weeds in thought's stream.
When the water flows more fully,
the husks, our ideas, pass along more quickly.
When this stream has become a torrent,
no care lingers in the mind of gnostics:
since the water has become so swift and full,
there is no longer room in it for anything but water.

8.

Tao Te Ching
8 Easy by nature

Lao Tzu
(500 B.C.)

True goodness
is like water.
Water's good
For everything.
It doesn't compete.

It goes right
to the low loathsome places,
and so finds the way.

For a house,
the good thing is level ground.
In thinking,
depth is good.
The good of giving is magnanimity;
of speaking, honesty;
of government, order.
The good of work is skill,
and of action, timing

No competition,
So no blame.

Taken from the Ursula K. Le Guin version

Tao Te Ching
15. People of power

Lao Tzu
(500 B.C.)

Once upon a time
people who knew the Way
were subtle, spiritual, mysterious, penetrating,
unfathomable.

Since they're inexplicable
I can only say what they seemed like:
Cautious, oh yes, as if wading through a winter river.
Alert, as if afraid of the neighbours.
Polite and quiet, like houseguests.
Elusive, like melting ice.
Blank like uncut wood.
Empty, like valleys.
Mysterious, oh yes, they were like troubled water.

Who can by stillness, little by little
make what is troubled grow clear?
Who can by movement, little by little
make what is still grow quick?

To follow the Way
is not to need fulfilment.
Unfulfilled, one may live on
needing no renewal.

Taken from the Ursula K. Le Guin version

10.

Tao Te Ching   Lao Tze
78 Paradoxes   (500 B.C.)

Nothing in the world
is as soft, as weak as water;
nothing else can wear away
the hard, the strong,
and remain unaltered.
Soft overcomes hard,
weak overcomes strong.
Everybody knows it,
nobody uses the knowledge.

So the wise say:
By bearing common defilements
you become a sacrificer at the altar of earth;
by bearing common evils
you become a lord of the world.

Right words sound wrong

Taken from the Ursula K. Le Guin version

11.

Haiku

Rain beats loudly down
Makes the trees bend their branches
Clouds empty. Who sees?

Dawne Kovan

12.

Tanka

Kyoto temple
Pebbles raked in swirling shape
Japanese garden
Master stands in pouring rain
Laughs as we run for cover.

Dawne Kovan

13.

Sacred Earth

The humanity of Earth
is a woven part
of our consciousness,
and of her Nature.
Without us, we would not "know"
That Earth is,
And Earth could not know
herself.

She sees herself in our eyes
as beautiful.
We stand on the seashore
and watch the waves
and know we are alive,
and Earth through us
knows her aliveness.
We know the morning birdsong
and the secret night,
and we give Earth back
her treasures.

So life dreams itself and
we dream Earth
in this unimaginable
Universe,
where infinity waits
for us to find ourselves

Maybe we are Earth's senses,
cells on her surface that tell her
what she is like;
where trees are, and ravines
and deep secret places,
white snows, eagle nests,
how it feels to walk barefoot
on her rain-drenched grass.

We sing the song of Earth
with our everyday being.
Be careful.
We are singing her dream
back to her
and we may sing her to sleep
or death.

Angela Locke

Crab Skeleton

blind brittle transparent
a binding between life and soul
animal and soul
the shadow thing
shadow of what was

this little life
the empty shells of eyes
bare-bleached   wind whitened

bone eyes stare sightlessly
endless tides and winds
wave-sucked have left
this sketch

skeleton of yourself I salute you
while all muscle marrow flesh rots
wind and sun take it
eviscerates dries bleaches flesh
falling clearly from the bone

all we are left with is the pattern
the bones hold
the shape
structures unfilled spaces empty eyes
shells scuttling cross empty seas

only my dreams of it
are held together
by this subtle sinew
shadow memory in a paper shape
parts so fragile a wind's breath will break

I hold this memory of life in my hand
blind eyes stare sightlessly back at me
I know all things in this moment
of Life's importance

the wind lifts the crab's skeleton
from my living palm
that bond of sinew
breaking into parts

brain eyes body are scattered
in the wind

to begin their turning into stars

Angela Locke

15.

Rose in Stone

These are life forms
the rose petal and the stone

rose petal pliant in the wind
easily bruised
it dies after a day's life
delicately veined, its heart's colour

drawn into its centre
open to the universe
it scatters scented messages for the bee

the bee does not come to the stone

stones are hard unyielding
if they give off scent
it is a distant air tang of the salt sea
in sun they hold heat

while petals wilt
beside me on the grass

our life is caught between them
the petal and the stone

stone
not so short as a flower's life
not so long as almost eternity

days and nights and seasons
aeons and epochs

deep deep time
these mark the turning of the stone
on the sea's bed

a loving and a working
in the deep slow time of the world
turning, caressing
the sea's fingers
on the seeming unchanging face of stone

until the sea finds
rest

stone stone
pebble pebble
tiny grain of sand
sand to atom atom to proton
into the secret heart of creation

where God may be

so we turn and turn

the atoms of the world in the sea's hand
in the wind's hand   in form and gravity
and fire
atom and atom   so we love
and from our loving

from the drawing of the deep earth place
some god   some creator
some mathematician
some star magician
draws down

the beginning
of the rose

Angela Locke

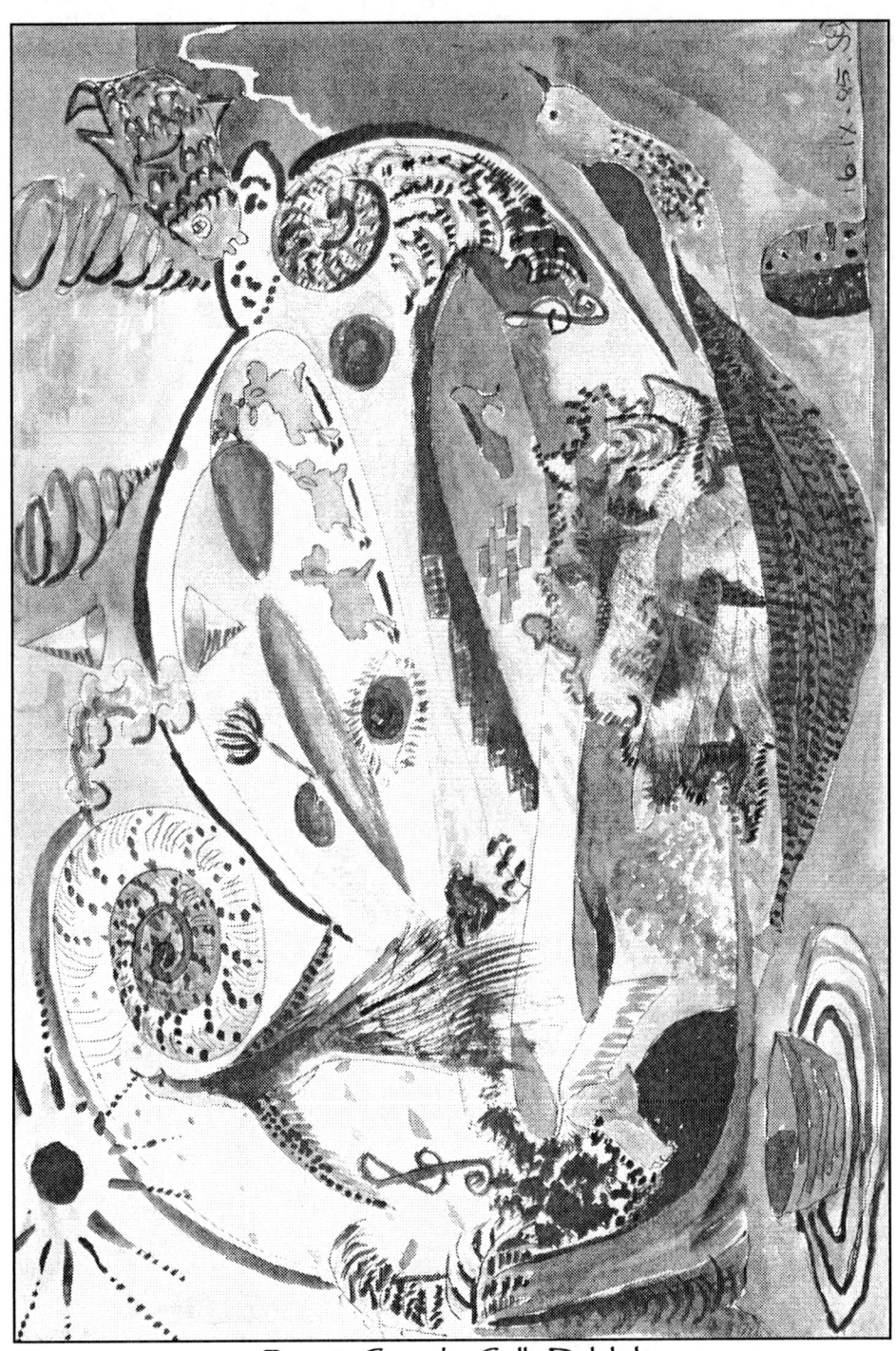

Rose in Stone by Sally Dalglish

16.

Iona

A rainbow beside the Abbey
links land and sky, island and mainland
where the houses left behind glow white
against a rain-rinsed sky.
Turquoise water and white sand
draw into each other,
separated, yet
(conjoined) by rock
the abbey stands in a plain space,
plainsong, stone, arch,
solidly upon the earth.

Something lifts us
as the soughing wind
creeps under oak doors
with a wild cry to the heart
and we think of doves in the morning
as the streamers of Easter tassels
stir in that old breeze.

Yet here is something new.
Across the Sound
the ferry cries as it beaches
like an old whale
who has lost her calf.

The old world is birthing
a new, bright morning
in this place.

Angela Locke

17.

Whales off the North beach : Iona

Companiably, quietly
they come together in blue water,
black, glossy tails glinting in sunlight.
Unhurried, exactly equidistant,
they stroll the sea
beyond the black rocks,
where surf threshes the edges of land.
Even across the distance of the bay
I hear them,
their inaudible whale language
their presence fills the bay
with silence and deep speech.
I am drawn into the circle of their being,
aware of the stillness,
creation weaving its web,
the rub of particle and molecule
between sea and land,
the endless sexual game of the and me
between edges, and frontiers
the journeys beteen,
the journey the sea makes, its language,
how we share its tides in our gut,
how these black-tailed whales
sing our songs,
dance our dance

We wave to one another
in our steady progress,
me in the hayfield above the machair,
they in their own place,
effortlessly, peacefully
cutting diamond water, while
simultaneously ruminating
on the state of the world
and rewriting Hamlet for whales.

Angela Locke

Earth Music

music is the breathing of the Earth
made Sound

the manifest Sound
of all unsounded things

light flickering on willow
damp woods
the mushroom touch of skin
lemondrop taste of windfall pears

even sounded things
taken beyond their Sound
are in this music

sighing trees in night winds
whispering waters
on a winter's marsh
the cry of geese flighting
the cry of children newly in the world

the cry of the hungry

sadness and joy
this is the music of the
living Earth

we cannot help but listen
recognising that this
is our music
and the breath
which gives us life

Angela Locke

19.

Himalayan Rainbow

We meet on the bridge between us
a rainbow arches over the valley
between mountain and mountain
this is the bridge
everything beneath is changed

we are linked for ever by this
the rainbow bridge
great mountains where gods live
a cherry tree lit by the morning sun

Angela Locke

20.

Bay Horse Farm

This is a slow place, climbing to the fell edge
where the light comes first in the morning.
Here yows mounting before the sun stand on skyline walls
At the world's end, and others sleeping in the pasture
Have faces white as old kings in marble.

This is the place of the curlew,
its call of the water source bubbling in the high meadow,
wings falling into the hollow sheep-backed
grass and here the walls are, for lambs to be on the wrong
side of, crying like human children,
and the yow answering at last with a throaty roar,
desperate and angry in the dark.

I know the night cry. I have felt
this loneliness for my children. These cries
disturb my sleep (I have stopped often
by the roadside to stuff hoggetts through hedges,
their black heads bunting mindlessly at gates
(which will not open) but in the dark
I too am helpless, and can only listen
to the cry.

If it weren't for cries like these, the night
would be perfect quiet, sweet starlight
and the smells of earth sweeping
in the fell wind, dung and grass
and river somewhere. I can sense them all,
and the dawn is only there, beyond the wall,
a little space away.

Angela Locke

Martindale Picnic

It is wonderful talk, full of us,
and such clever laughter funnels up the fulcrum of the rock
and bon mots and good companionship warm in the sun
with the wine cooled under moss and rock
and stream, there is a dream and all of us lever
in our own way, know what the world is,
I've seen it, I've seen it all, no, not seen it ALL,
still keep wondering, have a sense of wonder,
Isn't that important?

but one by one we slip away in silence,
one to climb the high side of the fell and one
the ravine, and one walks down the valley

and one is drench-eyed
on the high line of the crag riding the sky
this one backsides on to talk, how the wine falls away,
the snaked wall slithers up beyond, grey-blue mountains
are distant, still snow-flecked in June,
the whole nearness pattered with dung of fell ponies
 and the black-buttoned lumps of sheep dirt, and ponies stand
as plasticene models in a mock-up of a glacial valley,
only it's real, and you know it when you close your eyes
and the hush of river and sheep call weave across your dark.

Everything is impossibly high, peppered with wheeling crows,
Herdwicks and lambs black-faced Al Jolson,
and the yows sing back a gaunt-backed stomach-belching song

Will we meet together, knowing secrets lie in the speary
bog-grass, just there, just there, over the heart-thumping
tussocked hill, where the dry bedded stream once was,
just there where the sheep are only seen by us,
 and will we tell?

Angela Locke

22.

Disturbing the Heron

Old grey Sunday clerk is hunched up on the bridge,
coat wrapped firmly against the sun,
the wind plays in his sad feathers,
he watches fish flick and dance in the yellow water
dreaming of dinners he hasn't had.
From this height above the wood and stone
he is puffed-out puritan

no drink in this village, no dancing,
only the fish get away with it,
and I'll eat them before too long.

But we disturb his brooding as we run along the tawny riverside,
under the beech with the dogs.
And with a cry he is up, not the same bird,
he opens his coat into the sun,
great hoops of wings are kohl-edge maiden's eyes,
a long lightning zig of neck, elegance of beak
he hid before from us, he draws Chinese calligraphy of flight
through the blue afternoon, inches above the river.

The first moment he can settle a safe distance he comes down,
stands in the speared reed like the diva
surrounded by first soldiers, tufted head blending with shadows.

We see a ghost of him above the water, he is a creature of it,
only the water moves under him and he is still.

But as we watch, he darts his body in a fluid movement,
becoming the water in a flash of understanding,
and after a brief struggle, he is so still you dreamed it,
only now his fat-necked stance is saying one trout
isn't dancing any more.

Angela Locke

23.

Tarn

Tarns only are, darkish and mysterious
because hidden by mountains

we have to climb to them and arrive lacklustre
and the lustre of them is pearled on the still
surface and is deep in the rockfall
which plunges and steeps but is unmoved

in the deep where fish should not be but are
in the echo which disturbs
in the white flowers which stand like stars
above the water, in the plated slate stone
which waveless water does not wear away but goes on
not lack of clearness stops us seeing

when we can stop long enough from crackling
crisps and apples and sarnies, god how noisy we are
when we can stop long enough to feel the weight
of the stacked rock and the cupped sense of water
on old fires, where lava and volcanoes

were, the light comes, fish jump, how do they come,
this high? and there are miracles you would believe
because it is magic fay wild people fear these places
they are so silent when you speak it tumbrils round
and round and round
you think voices will avalanche the scree
they don't but something else falls away

silence we fear so much comes into us
a quiet of greenshadow under the fell and the sundialed sun
moves round again cragpointed by the reflected dark

we sit on the short grass
split from holes under the white rock
one to torment a wheatear's nest and one
comes slow and slow to us, until close it rests
its splayed hands on rock, pointed head
is chestnut fire, white bibbed, no baby this

we are afraid like the wheatear, the weasel stares,
Long light, Sun shifts above Nan Bield pass.
The deep deep place you can see when you go high
glitters. The eyed weasel glows against the stone;
for great seconds he watches us.

Peregrine, we know her neat,
stoops and cries above the fell. The weasel flicks
under a night stone.

Angela Locke

The Mist

Grey clouds engulf the darling vale
and gently shed their rain in drops
upon the earth.

A quiet now descends as evening settles in;
there's no discordant sound.
The river curves through banks of rhododendrons
while scarlet poppies stand up clear
against its darkening flood.

A breeze picks up and skims the surface making
a tracery of lines.
Swallows swerve and dip to catch elusive flies.
The beauty lingers on to deepen in the mind,
To carve eternal images that cannot be defined.

Mary E Burkett OBE

25.

The River Derwent

Flecks of light across the surface sparkling white.
flashing sun rays sending echoes back.
Swinging round Kirk Fort,
the swirling eddies push and pass,
forming a mass of fleeting patterns,
crossing, changing, intertwining,
coursing, playing, still careering on towards the sea.

Mary E Burkett OBE

26.

Driving over Dunmail after a storm

Look. Look, look at the hills!
They've burst into a thousand rills,
lining the bracken with white frills,
Flashing and frothing, the water spills,
down it tumbles in gallons and ghylls
while down below dry Thirlmere fills.

Mary E Burkett OBE

27.

Seascale

Silver light dapples the dashing breakers
as they surge towards the shore.
Silver clouds let rays through sparsely
as they slant to the ocean's floor.

A liquid, raging, foaming flood,
each wave competing with the next
to reach the pebble strewn beach.

But each, and each, is brought up short
as rampant horses when reined in.
They jostle, back, recede and stop;
their race is done.

Mary E Burkett OBE

We walk the land

We walk the land
We sing the land
We draw our alphabet from the land.

V is for Valley and vastness of space
M is for mountain, for moor and mount
W is for waves, waves of the sea

C is the crescent moon
O is the full
A is for awe and amen.

Y is the crooked Yew, the I, the you with arms outstretched

I is the stave that seeds the moon's O
S is for snake and the path we walk.

Geraldine Green

We Walk the Land by Sally Dalglish

I rescued four baby newts

Today I rescued four baby newts
they were in the back of the florists
she put them in a tin of water
and moss.
I carried them to a local pond
Jackson's pond
and got bitten by a horsefly
        possibly Jackson's horsefly.

Geraldine Green

30.

Remember the gods of small places

Remember the gods of small places
whose names we can't always remember
and remember them when we can
which isn't often.

We must remember the names of the little places
the ones that grace our memoirs
lace intricate knots
of not-understanding why we do what we do what we do what we

and remember the games played on the bank of the twelve swans
beneath the green barking of alders on the water's
banking sharply to meet

each with the other as we dipped our toes into mud
and thought it was clear
what we want and it is but it isn't

and Oxon, yes, Oxon should be a village that we
yes, should be a village that we make love in, amidst the spiralling
steam of a sweaty chimney lit against damp October days

as it
and the swan laze against the ripples.

Geraldine Green

In one field

In one field black sheep
in the other white
and a sign we didn't read,
saying 'closed'

on one bank moss-rocks,
on the other us
and a sign saying 'no entry'
or possibly 'forbidden',
that we ignored

and I remember your hand, brown
and mine pink and a parcel of swallows made up the sky

a dash of water please, just to make it fresh
a splash of sunlight shimmering on the freckled river, to send
it running
and I remember curled lashes framing hazel eyes,
yes, hazel eyes and clouds, always clouds through the sun
and my hands, brown now and yours pink.

Geraldine Green

I am Each of These by Sally Dalglish

Sal Madge

Each summer and winter like seabird returning
she'd follow the tideline from dawn until dusk,
glass bottles, old nets, dead fish she'd leave stranded,
her eyes trained only on coal and driftwood.

At night she'd walk back to Rosemary Lonnin'
to others a slum to Sal it was home
her feet she'd rest upon the brass fender
take out of her brat a clay pipe to suck on
lean into the fire with tongs take an ember
draw deep on her pipe close her eyes hum a song.

Wagon-tipped slack thrown down the steep slagheap –
she heard it again so deep was her sleep
she and her friends on the slurry-hill scrambled
for coal they called black-jack, hard nuggets of scrawn.

    Sal Madge? Yes she lived in Rosemay's Lonning,
    smoked a pipe wore men's britches and scratted for coal.

Geraldine Green

Tupping-time

Sharp tang of sheep dung
hung on damp air, tattered leaves,
thorn-clung scraps,
delicate, flung to earth.

Scenting ewes the tup turned,
curled his lip and sniffed.

Old, still used to the role,
he swaggered forward.

Rowans twisted over the gill,
dropped clear red berries
into full waters.

Clusters of Herdwicks
turned to stare,

coloured rump-rags told
of favours given, received,
withheld, seed spurted, swelled
within, awaiting spring.

Ravens passed over,
Scavengers of blood-soaked scraps
dropped, after birth.

Geraldine Green

Solway

Beyond Lugh's Chair the Plain of Solway
leaps to greet the salmon run
into nets across the Eden
where rivers meet the searing sun.

In the sound of seabirds crying
hear the clang of flashing blades
battles fought for land and favours
shape this troubled Solway Plain.

Breath of cattle, humans, seabirds,
drift the air in spiralled dreams,
ancient memories intermingle
with our own fragmented seams.

Flickering echoes, sand-drop, timeless,
shift and shimmer beyond Caerluel.
in Lugh's arms the gold-shaft quivered,
flashing, hissing, kissed the sea.

Geraldine Green

Watersmeet   16 March 2003

In water's spirit I am there
The hidden jewels of tender care
Use me, Drink me to cleanse your Soul
Through your visions you will know it all.

Dennis Irwin

Meeting of Magnificent and Delightful by Sally Dalglish

Free Spirit, High Flyer   February 2003
Written for a flying friend, Charles Dalglish

He's out in space among the clouds far out in the blue
His spirit soars and sails way beyond accounts and cares
Of gravity, earth, dust and poetry
In an environment which still grants the chance to dare:

An opportunity today so very scarce. Few
Can deliberately challenge life and fate
In competition within the sphere of earthly space, pulling out of
A screaming spin at an all impressive rate

Or yet on another "spree", feeling the need for private
thought
About things mysterious, ethereal, the need to be alone,
Needs that can only be satisfied in the secrecy of a cloud
Where such thought and feelings are destroyed by phones.

Thus enclosed in soft, enfolding and insulating cloud –
Again the challenge of the anaesthesia of space
Leading, if not careful, to the serendipity of permanent peace
Where he can cheerfully throw off the "coils" of the "race":

The race to compete in mortal things in life's striving for
success
But oh! what matters any such commercial things
While airborne soaring in angelic flight
Closeted in the seclusion of cloud supported wings!

At flight's conclusion to the safety of the "roost"
First to negotiate through the "goal posts": arrival safe
And, returning too the ground at "Hartley base"
Landing lights untouched, he's welcomed like a long lost waif.

Present now and not so quiet is a more recent chariot:
A Hugh's 500 whose gas turbine makes the rotors zing
A faint vibration . . . a bit of a shudder . . .
Some collective, a bit of rudder and lo! It takes to wing.

Vertical take - off what a thrill! An elevator with no shaft
Once again into the beckoning void of airy, misty blue
A heavenly platform revealing the all round scene
Then adroitly moving gently, softly to catch another view.

The spirit now contemplating age and flight
Has made provision by turning a brand new page
In manufacture subversive, secret a more docile
HOVERCRAFT is to create the latest rage.

Eventually, inevitably, the spirit will be brought to earth
And have to deal with things that cause real tension:
"Mow the lawn, take the garbage to the tip,"
Can only be mitigated by memories of the third dimension,

Flight.

To Sally: In scads of water you puts your trust,
But H2O turns ships to rust
To face the problems you have defined
You' be better served with a bottle of wine
MUDGEE of course!

With apologies to Pam Ayres

Mike Brown A.E.   Gulgong N.S.W. Australia

37.

In Memory of Alex Dalglish
who died before his time.

My tears flow.
How will I remember you?
Your eyes of crystal blue
That sparkled with intelligence,
Some-one of such diligence.

How will I remember you?
Sports-minded
Kind hearted,
The creator of a beautiful house,
A person of such nous
Especially when it came to cards
You always caught us off our guard.

How will I remember you?
You brought a lot of fun
To our Christmas in the sun
You played a great game of French cricket
And talk about artistic!

How will I remember you?
You were such a clever creator
When you put your pastels to paper
That's how I'll remember you:
You were special, one of a kind.

Faye Dalglish (niece), Brisbane   May, 2001

A time to grieve   1st January 2002

The river that is my soul is frozen.
It makes no progress, stilled by the wind of bitterness

But leave me now for I am wounded.
Tell me not to hide my grief, to make pretence of happiness.

For my soul needs this time of pain,
Until the angel of spring sheds warm, gentle tears into my heart.

Then the river will surely flow again,
A slow trickle building to a torrent of rage which brings relief;

Crashes against the rocks,
Shattering the torment, the hurt and despair like shards of ice

Then my soul will reach calm waters,
Flowing freely, gurgling and laughing, away from my frozen past.

Norma Gunn

Reflections and echoes

Are there mirrors in the stream?
Reflected I see blue sky, I see clouds, I see trees
What I fear is that I won't see me.

Is there an echo in this cave?
Listening I hear birds calling, I hear wind blowing
What I fear is that I won't hear me.

Is there recognition in this touch?
Feeling I sense a hand, I sense a face, I sense a presence
What I fear is that I won't sense me.

Am I real, do I exist
Do you see me, hear me, sense my nearness?
A reflection, an echo, a recognition of being –
That is me. I am.

Norma Gunn

Dark Horizon 13th September 2003

Dark, flat sea, deep and black
Dark sky above – and between –
Straight dark line which is the horizon
Straight dark line holding you to me.

Down and down, deeper
Touching ....? rock bottom
hard
unyielding
cutting.

Down again, searching beneath.

Finding .... ? fire – raging
hot
unquenchable
burning.

Fire explodes, turns rock to molten gold.

Bubbles of light prick the velvet sea.
Lightening the darkness on the horizon –
Straight silver line holding you to me.

Norma Gunn

Magic

There is a touch of magic
of healing in the air.
Singing birds are music
soft, sharp and very clear
Water still like glass
holds the secret wisdom
through which we all must pass.
The beauty of creation
surrounds us every day.
We fail to see its meaning
in all we do and say
Jesus' voice is calling – to
all who follow him:
"I am the source of freedom
through which your soul must pass."

Patricia Irwin

Aquifer

Aquifer, aquifer,
vital necessity,
friend when I'm thirsty and
foe when you flood
I am a child of the
Land that you water
I am a son of the
soil that you drain.

Aquifer, aquifer
Founder of Warfedale,
carving the crags with your
liquid so hard,
chiselling my heart with your
tools I can't see, you have
opened a way and flowed
into my soul.

Jonathan Atkinson

Rain

Floods come every year
Swept in front of the wind brushed
Rain
To fill the channels,
(Man-made take-aways)
Hewn through the fenlands
Damp and peaty.

Moss-filled
Brown earthed it seeks the sea
Again,
A prodigal long way,
To join the skipping waves
Where John lost the polished
Stones of state.

Drains feed into Nene by Tydd Gote
And on to Old Lynn Channel,
The Main
Awash with wind hurled water's rush,
From Mare's Tail shoal, and on
To Bulldog sands.
Receives its own again.

John Crossley

River of dreams

In the ding dong battle that is life
there are summer moods of peace and calm
when nature, man and beast are one,
and river's soft meanders run
in heavy silence broke by insects' hum
and an air filled and plump with
summer's richness after rain,
sun and shadow's leafy green.

How I could lie then in the tall grass
and listen to the chirps and chips of bird song
always clear and fresh however
long before begun.

Better still to enjoy the smell of new mown hay,
a soft bosom on which to rest my head,
and share dreams or quiet breath
in a free but stolen kiss,
and seal the unspoken promises of bright
but untutored eyes
with a poesy of summer's flowers.

Even now, the cornflower
radiant blue, lifts me, no matter
where I am, into warm and
memories deep of summer moods
when there was only river,
lanes and trees
and you and me.

Charles Gardiner

The Drowning

She lost her child in water.
He lost his mind for a while.

They hid their mighty anger
Till
it all
came out. It was
as a flood is, swelling
like a welling beck
that beckoned to the child
who drowned.

Slipped out of life as if
it was silk. Left lives
lined with silt.
Spilt them
at the whitewater.

Stopped
like broken
rafts
in
canyons.

She is a heaving cataract on the stairs.
His garden is an early grave.

Jane Moss-Luffrum

In Death We Reach All by Sally Dalglish

46.

Fewer Mouths

There are no goldfish in the tank –
We treat it as a water feature.
They all went furry, died and sank.
There are no goldfish in the tank,
Even the plastic plants look rank.
We've killed off every living creature;
There are no goldfish in the tank.
We treat it as a water feature.

Huw Evans

47.
The Colour of Sound

Cool, dark green
Basis for growth
Shot through with sparks
Where the gold threads peak

The cool green water
Placidly flowing
Tipped with gold as
The sunbeams pierce
The canopy of foliage

Sun is setting now
The water tinged with red
As it hurls itself
Over stones and falls
Crying, yet going on

Deep dark blue of night
Turning the water petrol
Slowly oozing
Melding, yielding,
Being embraced by the ocean

Becoming one with it
In the star-lit dark
Until the sun rises
And the golden kingdom is attained

Dorothy Chalk

The Monster Serpent

Out on the surface of the lake,
See those shifting humps appearing!
Up and down, along it travels,
Where's it come from? Where's it going?

Now its path curves nearer to us!
Blunt, small, bewhiskered head in front.
But see, each hump has head and tail!
Otters at play formed our serpent.

Dorothy Chalk

Pilgrimage

I did not choose to go on pilgrimage
Chosen, carried, led, directed, taken
When I perceived, eventually, the goal
I was able to claim it for my own

I still take side paths which lead me astray
But an innate sense of direction calls
Or my companions get too far away
And I slowly return to the true path

My pace adjusts to those with whom I go
For pilgrims form a welcome family
Who grow together as we travel on
And each contributes to the company

Along the way we learn to see the scene
To hear the praise of birds, or the silence,
The sound of water always catches me
The living water from the rocks of time

I pause to watch a tiny waterfall
Delighted in the colours of the moss
But entranced by the music I can hear
For I am musically illiterate

So I travel on, others come and go.
Moving slowly or leaving me behind
I know my goal and am thankful for friends
Who walk with me upon this pilgrimage.

Dorothy Chalk

Safe Harbour

The sea's salt kisses change the land.

Sometimes the scene is peace and calm.
Even then minute grains of sand,
Tiny rock chips move position,
Change their shape and alter others.

Sometimes the restless, rolling tide
Runs at the beach, which rattles back
In stony mirth, until they reach
Their joint compromise solution,
Wrestling amicably, changing.

Sometimes indeed, the sea's surge swells
Until, driven by wind and tide,
It ravages the cowering shore.
Its force removes ancient landmarks,
Rolls rocks and tree trunks like marbles,
Leaves deep love bites in land's soft line.

Note how solid water-worn cliffs
Stand firm on either side this bay.
Here see the spray spring rainbow-hued
Where the deep twisted fault lines link
Turbulent sea to the still sky.
Pebbles, a shingle bar and sand
Lie quietly, a safe harbour.

Our human tenancy's short span
Sees boat of skin or chunky wood,
Heart-of-oak vessel, craftsmen made,
Or modern shipyard masterpiece,
Paddled, sailed, motor-driven,
Scud before the storm to safety
Within this sanctuary, where
  The sea's salt kisses change the land.

Dorothy Chalk

What Do We Hear?

Earth speaks: – what do we hear?
We hear our own pulse
the air entering and leaving our body
the friction of our skin with itself and other things
the ting of a nail on metal
the slap of a flat hand – we hear our own voice
other voices, loved or hated
or tolerated
we hear each other...

Earth speaks : what do we hear?
We hear the cry of seagulls
following the plough
and its tractor
we hear the growl of bulldozer
the rattle of soil and stones
that it drops
we hear the sound of landslide
rock on rock, trees crackling
the land moving...
we hear
the rasp of blowing sand
the glop of mud hole geysers
the sizzle of molten lava
The land speaks...

Earth speaks: – what do we hear?
The murmur of the breeze in the grass

the roar of the wind in the trees
the thunder of the storm...
the song of the desert wind
the scream of the hurricane
the moan of the polar wind
the air speaks...

Earth speaks: - what do we hear?
The crackle of paper and sticks | the hearth
the friendly hum and pop as it burns
the blaze and crash of the bonfire
the painful bangs of a house ablaze
the smouldering growl of a fire in peat and
the exploding leaps of a gum forest fire
fire speaks

Earth speaks: - what do we hear?
The drip of a tap
the ripple of a burn
the chatter of a stream
the grumble of a river
the sigh of the sea on the shore
the sound of the surf
the crash of the wave...
the groan of the glacier
the gulp of the whirlpool
the creaking of the ice flows
water speaks
Earth speaks: - what do we hear?

Dorothy Chalk

52.

Green Chakra

The green of my garden,
The green of my heart.
Earthed in the turf, spring grass spears through.
Apple leaves shelter pink-tipped blossom,
Unconditional love.
My emerald ring, round-shaped for eternity,
Remembrance of lily in Irish garden.
Jade beads like threaded hellebores,
Sculpted lotus and celadon vase.
Calm sea, aquamarine and turquoise,
Bottle-nosed dolphins in bottle-green deep water.
Tree ferns stretch like feathers in flight,
Ancient trees reach for the sunlight
Crowned by gold in Autumn days.
I sit in my garden remembering.

Jill Jackson

53.
Regeneration

The Mute Swan sings but once before she dies
The legend goes.
I watched her flying in
From far off mountains
To the mirror lake.
Reflections grey and still
From rocky cliffs,
And coloured bands
From flowers so close to shore.
The centre of pure azure
From the sky above
She stretched her feet
And then with folding wings
Settled in the circle.
Lifting her graceful neck
She uttered this unearthly cry
Of exultation and despair,
Then sank beneath water.
I watched from the shore.
A brilliant flash.
A jewel of malachite, cobalt, turquoise
Rose from the centre.
A tiny Kingfisher sped
Towards the distant river.
The Humming birds, changed from humble Sparrows
Were feeding on the flowers around my feet.
I turned to go.
My time had not yet come.

Jill Jackson

The Pull of Water

We are an island people.
We know the pull of water
That goes away to horizons unknown.

As we stand on the shores of this inland water –
Surrounded by mountains – contained,
We feel the pulse of its tranquillity.

It is the very containment that delights,
Gives us renewed calm to go on,
Despite all that the outside world has spoilt.

We send our thoughts
Skittering over the surface
Like flat ones – yet making no indent.

We only know the quiet that holds us
Is constant – giving us hope for all mankind
In its serenity and strength.

Because we feel the deep pull of water

Hazel Lee

The Pull of Water by Sally Dalglish

Inside the Shell   15th April 2002

Sitting in my giant shell
I hear the booming ocean.
Waves roar like lions
echoing in hollow chambers.
Surf rides basalt rocks
and sea horse spray rears up,
then crashes down, pounding stone to sand.
Ripples shimmer on frosted glass
like several shoal of mackerel.
Out at sea, a surge of mercury
rumbles over ridge and boulder
while on the shore, frothy waves
like hems of lace, tickle shell sand.
Kelp, dripping, laid out like laundry
mingles, with girls lost crimson ribbon.
Empty crab case, mermaids purse
lie abandoned on the shingle.

Limpets, flecked with foam do cling
a gull glides by on angled wings
and screams
Below the ceaseless lapping tide
from turquoise blue turns aquamarine.
Flung from mental fetters ... free!
I take one lemming leap.
For safe inside my spiral shell
I can see the sea.

Alicia Lester

Water of Life April 2003

Water of Life,
Pouring down from the sky
Tumbling down from rocks on high,
Flowing into river and stream
Gushing from taps that gleam,
Rushing onwards to the sea,
Water of Life,
Forms a large part of me.

Margaret Morton

The Sea

Thy tapestry should be sewn with silk, for sheen,
with iridescent turquoise, jade and cloudy green.
This is the sea, recurring motif
in the pattern of my life,
governed by lunar magnetism:
free of computer,
of any machinations of man;
infallible.

My life is like the Great Sea –
its heaving power both daunts and compels me.
Yet my strength of intellect, my tide of emotion,
ebbs and flows in a pattern immutable
yet unique to my personality.
I have learnt when to swim,
when float with the tide
and to accept myself.

I would not walk the shore of life,
only paddling in the shallows a spectator,
unwilling to step out of my depth.

I am aware of others, more brave,
who fling themselves into the yeasty breakers,
exhilarated by its depth, its power.
Beyond the terror of the first overwhelming roller,
they find a buoyant balance and a rocking security.

O mastery of the deeps!

What of those tempted to venture farther,
to sail beyond the sunset and the western stars,
who disappear from our sight?

Like children left forlorn, we grieve for those
who have gone.
Yet somewhere beyond our sight
they make landfall on a spiced shore,
where falls neither rain, nor bitter snow,
the sun is gentle
and the winds are
still.

Vi Taylor

Archaeologists' Report: 4000 A.D.　　　April 2003

From the old riverbed
we excavated layers of silt
and in the lower layer
a collection of ritual objects
was found.

They are made of thin metal
(See Appendix A)
woven into a loose mesh
with traces of rudimentary wheels
they could be pushed or pulled
by hand, but not easily.

Obviously
they could have no practical purpose
in an aquatic setting.

We think they were offerings
perhaps associated with sacrifice
(Though no trace remains of this)
to a river deity
called Safeway.

Our colleagues found in a lake
(See Appendix B)
similar ritual objects
dedicated to Tesco.

Ann Ward

Sea Beast

The Sea Beast sways in the sun
And licks his prey,
Curling his tongue around the rocks,
He dribbles in anticipation of the feast to come
And foaming saliva spray
Slides down back into himself.
He gently mauls the stones
Rolling them over in his mouth
Then letting them go
Only to draw them back.
His captive rock-prey can only wait
To be slowly shaped by his hunger –
Sucked and bitten into his fantasy.
He taunts the sand – pushing it away
Then clawing it back.
Today he is almost benign
Waving to the seaweed below,
But he is only softening her up
To be devoured at his leisure.

Sylvia Stevens

Aira Force

Waterfall,
immense, irresistible force
stilled for a short breath of time
by a power greater than your own.
The chill of winter has frozen you,
static immobile,
your energy conquered,
your moving, tumbling water suspended
in solid ice.
waiting for spring to release you,
when slowly the thaw begins.
The drip, the crack,
as chunks of ice fall away,
to allow the flow, the surging power
of an endless cycle.
Once more you begin
your journey to the distant ocean.
From there to return again
In clouds
To fall as rain
Upon the mountain top.

Elizabeth Josh

Memory

I have a memory in my mind
of darkly rushing water.
Swirling leaves, tumbling sticks, foam
and fury beneath my feet.
"Don't fall in!"

I have a memory in my mind
of gentle, tranquil water.
Sunlight glinting, goldfish drifting, lily-pads
and softly murmuring wind.
"Don't fall in!"

I have a memory in my mind
of king-fisher blue
A sudden flash of colour, deeply embedded,
that memory has lasted a lifetime long.
"Don't fall in!"

Why don't they stop? I'm not a fool
to forget or ignore their care for me.
Just leave me standing on the bridge
whilst memory of beauty lingers in my mind.
"Don't fall in!"

Elizabeth Josh

The Quiet Pool

Tranquil pool
gold, amber and deep translucent brown
white water lily
green grassy banks with overhanging branches
of golden willow
quiet haven past which tumbles the busy river,
river in spate,
skipping over stones
rushing past rocks
gushing, swirling its way to ...
where?

The quiet pool ponders
this babble and turmoil
what is it about?

Likewise
the river marvels at the patience of
that gentle stillness -
it glimpses great beauty
in the serenity, and wonders if its own
rush and turmoil will ever cease
whether one day
it will itself find peace.

E A Josh

Raindrops on the Window

I am the raindrop on the window
I am the pebble on the seashore.
The flowers at my feet are part of me.
The trees were here before me and will
live long after I am forgotten but
I am the trees and they are me.

Shy little birds and ferocious beasts
are part of I am just as I am
the Lion that eats the Lamb that eats
the Grass and so my consciousness
spreads and envelopes all that is
and has been and will be.

No separateness exists though I think
it does until I look and see how
nothing can be separate as all is one,
all is energy and that energy is
the Source of All.

E. A. Josh

The Stream Spoke to Me

18 October 2000

Swirling! Rushing! Angry!

Why are you angry, dear water?

All water is one, each drop is part of the whole.
I fall from the sky, live in the ocean or
exist deep underground in the
Rock of the planet.
Why am I angry, you ask?
How can you ask!
Think what your kind are doing to me,
The poisons you pour into my being.
How can I not be angry.
Your kind seem amazed at my anger
as I flood your lands and destroy
your cities.
How can I not be angry
At what you do to me,
The source of your own being
And your sustenance.

Elizabeth Josh

The Plight of Water by Sally Dalglish

Printed in the United Kingdom
by Lightning Source UK Ltd.
100698UKS00001B/63-78